BILLING PHYSICIAN SERVICES

PROVIDED BY NURSE PRACTITIONERS

in Offices, Hospitals,

Nursing facilities, Homes and Hospice

Law office of Carolyn Buppert, P.C.
7972 Old Georgetown Road
Bethesda, MD 20814
www.buppert.com
Telephone 301-656-2287

BILLING PHYSICIAN SERVICES

PROVIDED BY NURSE PRACTITIONERS

in

Offices

Hospitals

Nursing facilities

Homes

Hospice

Carolyn Buppert

This publication is designed to provide accurate and authoritative information regarding the subject matter covered. It is sold with the understanding that the publisher is commenting only on the situations described herein, and is not providing legal advice to individuals whose situations differ from the examples addressed in the book. If legal advice or other expert assistance is required by a reader, the services of a qualified attorney should be sought. Sound legal advice depends upon an analysis of the facts specific to a situation, analysis of relevant state and federal law, and an application of the facts of a situation to the law.

ISBN 978-0-9818481-3-6
Library of Congress Control Number 2009911275

Carolyn Buppert
Law Office of Carolyn Buppert
7972 Old Georgetown Road
Bethesda, MD 20814
Telephone 301-656-2287
Web site: www.buppert.com

CONTENTS

PREFACE

Nurse practitioners have the qualifications and legal authority to perform clinical health and illness services, some of which are defined as physician services, billable to third-party payers.

How does a nurse practitioner get reimbursed for his or her services? The answer depends upon the following factors:

- State law regarding the scope of practice, definition and qualifications of a nurse practitioner
- The payer (Medicare, Medicaid, commercial indemnity insurers or managed care organizations)
- The setting (hospital, nursing home, office, or patient's home)
- Policies of commercial insurers, health plans, health maintenance organizations and managed care plans
- The services the nurse practitioner is performing.

An additional consideration is the employment or contractual arrangement between nurse practitioner and a group, a facility or an individual physician. In states where physician collaboration is not mandated and in a practice where no patients are covered by Medicare, a nurse practitioner may have a solo practice, with no business or working relationship with a physician, other than to give or take referrals. In that case, the nurse practitioner's reimbursement from third-party payers is going to depend on state Medicaid policy and the policies of commercial payers, which vary from state to state and from rural to urban area.

While some nurse practitioners are self-employed, and have no business or legal relationship with a physician, most nurse practitioners practice in some business relationship with a physician, a group or other provider entity. Generally, the relationships fall into one of four models:

- Nurse practitioner practice with off-site collaborating physician
- Nurse practitioner practice within a physician practice
- True team (medical doctor and nurse practitioner share the responsibility for care of patients)
- Physician with nurse practitioner assistant

For each of these models, the legal requirements, working relationship, business relationship, reimbursement implications, malpractice liability implications and patient perception are summarized.

Nurse practitioner practice with off-site collaborating physician

Legal requirements: Some states, and Medicare, require nurse practitioners to have a physician collaborator. Collaboration means slightly different things in different states and under Federal law. Federal law defines collaboration as:

> a process in which a nurse practitioner works with a physician to deliver health care services within the scope of the practitioner's professional expertise, with medical direction and appropriate supervision as provided for in jointly developed guidelines or other mechanism as defined by the law of the State in which the services are performed. 42 U.S.C.S. §1395x(aa)(6).

The collaborator's physical presence is not required by law. The collaborator may be off-site most or all of the time. Usually, a collaborator agrees to be available for consultation with a nurse practitioner, either in person or by telecommunications. Usually, the collaboration requirement is memorialized through a written agreement between the nurse practitioner and medical doctor.

Working relationship: The communication between physician and nurse practitioner may be frequent, infrequent or varying in intensity, depending upon the issues which arise.

Business arrangement: The collaborator generally has no financial interest in the nurse practitioner's practice. The nurse practitioner usually pays the collaborator a set annual or monthly fee, an hourly rate, or some combination of set fee and hourly rate. Occasionally, the medical doctor serves as and is titled as medical director of the nurse practitioner's practice.

Reimbursement implications: Medicare and Medicaid directly reimburse nurse practitioners who perform medically necessary physician services and who have their own practices, with off-site physician collaborators. Commercial payers make their own rules. Some reimburse nurse practitioners practicing under this model; others reimburse physicians only.

Who patients see: Patients see only the nurse practitioner.

Malpractice liability: In general, a collaborating physician is assigned no malpractice liability for a nurse practitioner's mistakes, unless the nurse practitioner consulted the collaborator regarding the injured patient, and the collaborator's advice did not meet the standard of care.

Nurse practitioner practice within a physician practice

Legal requirements: All states authorize nurse practitioners to practice within a group of medical doctors.

Working relationship: A nurse practitioner handles his or her own panel of patients within a physician practice.

Business arrangement: The practice may pay the nurse practitioner an hourly rate, a set salary, a percentage of collections, a set salary plus a bonus, or the nurse practitioner may individually receive all collections attributable to his or her activities and may pay the practice a fee for rent and services provided. The nurse practitioner may be an employee of the practice, an independent contractor, or an employee leased from another practice or facility. The nurse practitioner often has no equity interest in the medical doctor's practice and does not participate in practice governance. If there is an employment relationship, the nurse practitioner reassigns reimbursements to the practice.

Reimbursement implications: All payers reimburse for physician services provided by nurse practitioners working under this model.

Who patients see: Patients might never see anyone but the nurse practitioner. Or, patients may see a physician occasionally.

Malpractice liability: If a nurse practitioner does not consult a physician, a patient is injured and the nurse practitioner has not met the standard of care, it is unlikely that a physician in the same practice would be held liable for the nurse practitioner's mistake. However, in many practices, nurse practitioners and physicians are covered under the same insurance policy. A damage award against a nurse practitioner may affect the group's rate.

True team

Legal implications: All states authorize nurse practitioners to practice within a team which includes physicians.

Working relationship: Clinicians consider all patients to be patients of the practice, facility or team, and communication varies depending upon the personalities and styles of the clinicians and the mix of patients.

Business relationship: The nurse practitioner and physician may share in practice equity and practice or facility governance, or not. Any business relationship agreeable to the parties and permitted by state law is possible.

Reimbursement implications: All payers reimburse for physician services provided by nurse practitioners working under this model.

Who patients see: Patients see a mix of clinicians.

Malpractice liability: The group or facility, as well as the individuals involved, likely would bear responsibility for a mistake by one of it's team members.

Physician with nurse practitioner assistant

Legal implications: All states authorize nurse practitioners to practice as an assistant to a medical doctor.

Working relationship: The physician sees all patients. The nurse practitioner sees some or all patients. For example, the nurse practitioner may take the history, perform the examination, establish the differential diagnosis, develop a treatment plan and write the progress note. The physician may see the patient, confirm or add to the nurse practitioner's findings and plan, and discuss the plan with the patient.

Business relationship: The medical doctor usually employs the nurse practitioner.

Reimbursement implications: All payers reimburse for physician services provided by nurse practitioners working under this model.

Who patients see: Patients usually identify the medical doctor as their clinician, but may see a nurse practitioner from time to time.

Malpractice liability: The medical doctor is likely to be liable for any breaches of the standard of care, as he or she is involved in the care of all patients.

CHAPTER 1

BILLING NURSE PRACTITIONER SERVICES
WHERE TO FIND THE RULES

Medicare

Medicare's rules for billing and coding medical visits in offices and clinics, patient's home, nursing facilities, hospitals and hospice are found scattered throughout the Federal law. Among the sources one must check when answering a question about this subject are:

- Chapter 42 of the *United States Code*
- Chapter 42 of the *Code of Federal Regulations*
- the *Medicare Claims Processing Manual*
- the Center for Medicare and Medicaid Services "Documentation Guidelines for Evaluation and Management Services"
- *Current Procedural Terminology*
- occasional Medicare program transmittals and
- local medical review policy documents.

To answer a question concerning services performed in nursing facilities, the patient's home or a hospital, consult these additional resources:

United States Code
http://www.gpoaccess.gov/uscode

Code of Federal Regulations
http://www.gpoaccess.gov/cfr

Medicare Manuals
http://www.cms.hhs.gov/Manuals

Hospital, Home Health and Skilled Nursing Facility Manuals
http://cms.hhs.gov/manuals/

Program transmittals
http://cms.hhs.gov/manuals/

Local Medicare Review Policies
Visit the web site of the local Medicare carrier

Documentation Guidelines
http://www.cms.hhs.gov/MedlearnProducts/20_ DocGuide.asp

Medicare's rules are the most detailed and accessible of any of the third-party payers. Virtually all of Medicare's rules and policies are available on-line. To stay up-to-date, sign up for a list-serve through the Center for Medicare and Medicaid Services (CMS) web site (www.cms.gov). List serve members are notified of changes in rules.

Medicaid

Medicaid's rules differ from Medicare's rules. Federal laws regarding Medicaid are found in:

Code of Federal Regulations
http://www.gpoaccess.gov/cfr

Medicaid is administered by the states. Regulations vary considerably from state to state regarding the billing of nurse practitioner services. Medicaid's rules are available from the state agency responsible for administering Medicaid.

Commercial indemnity insurers

Each commercial insurer makes its own rules, subject to state law addressing indemnity insurers. Commercial insurers may adopt Medicare's rules and guidelines on billing nurse practitioner services, or may adopt completely different policies. Each practice must query each insurer about the insurer's policies regarding reimbursement for services provided by nurse practitioners. Practice managers may find it useful to prepare grids which track the various insurers' policies. An example of such a grid is:

BILLING OF NP SERVICES

INSURER	BILL UNDER PHYSICIAN'S NAME	BILL UNDER NP'S NAME
XYZ	X	
ABC		X

and so on...

Commercial managed care organizations

Commercial MCO policies on reimbursement of nurse practitioners' services vary. Each commercial insurer makes its own rules, subject to state law addressing managed care organizations, health plans and/or health maintenance organizations. Each practice must query each managed care organization, health plan or health maintenance organization about the company's policies regarding reimbursement for services provided by nurse practitioners. Practice managers may find it useful to prepare grids which track the various insurers' policies. See example above.

Access to commercial payers' policies and rules

Certain commercial payers, such as Blue Cross and Aetna, publish some of their policies on-line. In general, however, a clinician must query an individual commercial payer as to its policies. It is safest to get the policies in writing. Commercial payers' policies may or may not be similar to Medicare policies.

Reimbursement levels and limitations

Medicare

Medicare pays nurse practitioners 85% of 80% of the Physician Fee Schedule rate for the CPT code billed, as long as no other provider has billed or been paid for the service. Medicare pays physicians 80% of the Physician Fee Schedule rate. The patient pays 20% of that rate—the "co-pay." Source: 42 USC 1395K(a) and 42 CFR 414.56. The Physician Fee Schedule rate varies from location to location and specialty to speciality. The schedule is available from local Medicare Carriers.

Medicare pays for services provided incident to a nurse practitioner's services, as well as the nurse practitioner's services. Source: 42 CFR 405.520 and 410.75.

Nurse practitioners must accept assignment; i.e. must accept the Medicare allowed charge amount as payment in full, requiring no additional payment from the patient, other than the co-payment amount. Source: *Medicare Claims Processing Manual*, Chapter 1, Section 30.3.1

Medicare will pay only the nurse practitioner, the nurse practitioner's employer, or an entity to whom the nurse practitioner has reassigned rights under a contract, under the rules on reassignment. Source: *Medicare Claims Processing Manual*, Chapter 1, Section 30.2.1

Medicaid

Federal law requires that the states:

(a) Provide that nurse practitioner services are furnished to the categorically needy.

(b) Specify whether those services are furnished to the medically needy.

(c) Provide that services furnished by a nurse practitioner, regardless of whether the nurse practitioner is under the supervision of, or associated with, a physician or other health care provider, may—

    (1) Be reimbursed by the State Medicaid agency through an independent provider agreement between the State and the nurse practitioner; or

    (2) Be paid through the employing provider. Source: 42 CFR 441.22.

Federal law mandates that states reimburse family nurse practitioners and pediatric nurse practitioners for services provided to patients covered by Medicaid, but does not mention adult nurse practitioners, geriatric nurse practitioners or nurse practitioners with other specialties. Source: 42 CFR 440.166.

States may elect to broaden federal law and reimburse adult nurse practitioners and geriatric nurse practitioners as well as pediatric and family nurse practitioners. Some states have elected to reimburse all types of nurse practitioners and other states reimburse only pediatric nurse practitioners and family nurse practitioners.

Fee-for-service Medicaid

A nurse practitioner who has a Medicaid provider number may bill Medicaid on a fee-for-service basis for physician services provided to a patient covered by Medicaid, if the patient is not enrolled with a managed care plan. In most states Medicaid pays nurse practitioners 100% of the physician's fee. In some states, Medicaid reimburses nurse practitioners at a reduced rate. For the rate in a state, contact the local Medicaid agency.

Medicaid managed care

If a patient is enrolled with a Medicaid managed care plan, the plan's policies and contracts will determine who may be reimbursed for physician services and the rate and form of payment. In general, managed care plans reimburse only those providers admitted to the plan's provider panel, and only those services authorized by the patient's primary care provider.

Medicaid managed care organization (MCO) policies on impanelment of nurse practitioners vary, and include admitting nurse practitioners to provider panels and declining to admit nurse practitioners to provider panels but allowing nurse practitioners to provide services for patients on a physician's panel. Reimbursement may be fee-for-service or a capitated rate.

A practice wishing to have a nurse practitioner admitted to a managed care provider panel must query the managed care plan regarding its policies. The credentialing and impanelment process takes 4 to 12 months.

Commercial indemnity insurers

Indemnity insurers reimburse health care providers on a fee-for-service basis. Each company has its own policies and fee schedules. Some companies' policies provide for reimbursing nurse practitioners' services at the same rate as physicians' services. Others reimburse nurse practitioners' services at a rate higher or lower than physicians. Some companies require that nurse practitioners and physicians be admitted to a provider panel; others do not. Some companies want nurse practitioner-provided services billed under a physician employer's name; others want nurse practitioners' services billed under the nurse practitioners' names. Some companies deny payment for services provided by nurse practitioners. Some states' laws require commercial indemnity insurers to reimburse nurse practitioners for physician services. Other states' laws are silent on the matter.

Commercial managed care organizations

In general, managed care organizations (MCOs) reimburse only those providers admitted to the plans' provider panels. MCOs do not admit all physicians to provider panels and may or may not admit nurse practitioners to provider panels. Commercial MCO policies on impanelment of nurse practitioners vary, and include admitting nurse practitioners to provider panels, declining to admit nurse practitioners to panels but allowing nurse practitioners to provide services for patients on a physician's panel, declining to admit nurse practitioners to provider panels, and permitting only those on providers panels to see patients.

Some MCO contracts allow the impaneled physician to delegate to his or her employees the authority to provide services but want services billed under the impaneled physician's name, no matter who performed the service. Other contracts are silent on delegation. Some contracts may require that the impaneled physician provide the physician services. If so, an MCO may consider it fraud for someone other than the impaneled physician to provide physician services.

If an MCO will not credential a group's nurse practitioners, and if the contract between MCO and the practice is silent on the issue of delegating the care of patients to a nurse practitioner, and if the practice intends to offer care by nurse practitioners to an MCO's patients,

then the practice should ask the MCO for written authorization, as part of the contract or by separate document, for nurse practitioners to provide services and receive reimbursement at the same rate as physicians.

Fee schedules vary from company to company and location to location, and are negotiable.

Minimum requirements for billing nurse practitioner services to third party payers

Practices, individuals, institutions or facilities must meet the following general requirements to bill a nurse practitioner's services to a third-party payer:

1. The services provided and billed are those that can be defined as physician services, as compared with nursing services or social work services. Federal regulations define physician services as diagnosis, therapy, surgery, consultation, and home, office and institutional visits.

2. The nurse practitioner has been credentialed as a provider, if a payer requires such credentialing, according to the payer's rules or policies.

3. The nurse practitioner meets the qualifications of a nurse practitioner, under the state's laws and the payer's policies.

4. The services the nurse practitioner performs are within the scope of practice for a nurse practitioner under the law of the state where the nurse practitioner performs the service.

5. The nurse practitioner has a physician collaborator if required by state law or if the payer is Medicare.

6. The service is medically necessary.

7. The service is documented appropriately.

8. The service is coded appropriately.

9. The provision of service is consistent with the laws regarding the setting where services are provided.

10. The service is not excluded under the terms of the patient's insurance policy.

Medicare has the following additional requirements:

1. The nurse practitioner accepts assignment; i.e. accepts the payment from Medicare as full payment.

2. The service is billed under name/number of individual providing the service.

3. If a consultation, there is an order for consultation. Note: As of press time, CMS had proposed to discontinue payment for the CPT codes for consultation.

4. The nurse practitioner has a collaborating physician of record.

5. The nurse practitioner has not been barred from participation in Medicare or another Federal program.

6. The payment is made in accordance with Medicare's rules on reassignment.

7. The nurse practitioner agrees to stay informed of and follow Medicare's rules.

8. The nurse practitioner is certified by a national certifying body.

9. The nurse practitioner has completed the application process and has a Medicare provider number.

Sources: Various sections of *The Code of Federal Regulations*, the *Medicare Claims Processing Manual* and the CMS 855 form.

Frequently asked questions

What are physician services?

A physician service is a service which can be described by a CPT code and justified by an ICD code.

Physician services include diagnosis, therapy, surgery, consultations and home, office and institutional calls. (Source: 42 CFR §410.20)

Current Procedural Terminology (CPT) lists procedure codes for all physician services. International Classification of Diseases (ICD) lists codes for diagnoses made by a physician.

What do the States authorize a nurse practitioner to do?

For the scope of practice in each state, see the Nurse Pracitice Act, accessible through the State Board of Nursing website.

What are the qualifications of a nurse practitioner?

Medicare

In order for Medicare Part B to cover a nurse practitioner's services, Medicare requires the nurse practitioner to:

- Be a registered professional nurse who is authorized by the State in which the services are furnished to practice as a nurse practitioner in accordance with State law; and

- Be certified as a nurse practitioner by a recognized national certifying body that has established standards for nurse practitioners or

- Have a Master's Degree in nursing. Source 42 CFR 410.75.

The following organizations are recognized as national certifying bodies:

- American Academy of Nurse Practitioners
- American Nurses Credentialing Center
- National Certification Corporation for Obstetric, Gynecologic and Neonatal Nursing Specialities
- Pediatric Nursing Certification Board
- Oncology Nurses Certification Corporation

- AACN Certification Corporation
- National Board on Certification of Hospice and Palliative Nurses

  Source: *Medicare Benefit Policy Manual*, Chapter 15, Section 200.

Medicaid

Medicaid requires a nurse practitioner to:

- Be a registered professional nurse who meets a State's advanced educational and clinical practice requirements, if any, beyond the 2 to 4 years of basic nursing education required of all registered nurses.
- Be currently licensed to practice in the State as a registered professional nurse
- Meet the State requirements for qualifications of pediatric nurse practitioners or family nurse practitioners in the State in which he or she furnishes the services or, if there are no specific qualifications for a pediatric or family nurse practitioner in the State, meet the qualifications for nurses in advanced practice or general nurse practitioners as defined by the State and
- Have a pediatric nurse practice or family nurse practice limited to providing primary health care to persons less than 21 years of age, in the case of a pediatric nurse practitioner, or limited to providing primary health care to individuals and families in the case of a family nurse practitioner. Source: 42 CFR 440.166.

States

The law of each State regarding the qualifications of a nurse practitioner is found in the State's Nurse Practice Act, accesible through the State Board of Nursing web site.

What are the requirements for physician collaboration in each state?

Collaborative requirements for nurse practitioners are found in the State's Nurse Practice Act.

When are nurse practitioner services not reimbursed under Medicare?

There are exceptions to the general rule that physician services provided by nurse practitioners are reimbursable. These exceptions are as follows:

1. Services to patients enrolled in hospice. See Chapter 6.
2. Admission evaluation to patients in skilled nursing facility services. See Chapter 4.
3. Monthly comprehensive evaluation of patients in skilled nursing facilities. See Chapter 4.
4. Certification and recertification of patients for home care. See Chapter 5.

Can a nurse practitioner perform and bill a consultation?

Yes. A nurse practitioner may request a consultation and may perform consultations when the performance is within the scope of practice for a nurse practitioner under state law. Source: *Medicare Claims Processing Manual*, Section 30.6.10. Note: As of January 2010, Medicare has decided to discontinue payment for the CPT codes for consultations.

How do I bill patient teaching?

When more than half of the time spent during a face-to-face visit is spent on counseling, a nurse practitioner or physician may bill on the basis of time spent. Select an evaluation and management code which corresponds to the total time of the face-to-face visit. Codes and corresponding times are found in *Current Procedural Terminology*.

Examples of counseling are:

- giving diagnostic results, impressions and/or recommended diagnostic studies;
- discussing prognosis;
- discussing risk and benefits of treatment options;
- giving instructions for treatment and/or follow-up;
- discussing the importance of compliance with chosen treatment options;
- discussing how to reduce risk factors;
- educating patients and families.

Example: If a face-to-face office visit with an established patient is 40 minutes, and 21 minutes of that time is spent on counseling, bill a level 5 visit. Current Procedural Terminology states, in the description of a level 5, established patient office visit: "Physicians typically spend 40 minutes face-to-face with the patient and/or family."

Document the length of time of the encounter and the subject matter discussed. If history-taking, physical exam, and medical decision-making are performed, document those things as well. Source: "Documentation Guidelines for the Evaluation and Management Codes," 1997, Center for Medicare and Medicaid Services.

When billing commercial insurers, do we bill the nurse practitioner's services under the physician's name and/or provider number?

If a practice's contract with a commercial payer has no specific prohibitions on nurse practitioners performing physician services, and no reimbursement differential between physicians and nurse practitioners, many practices bill nurse practitioners' work under a physician's name. Some commercial payers tell practices to bill a

nurse practitioner's services under a collaborating physician's name or provider number. This directive directly conflicts with Medicare's policy, which requires that services be billed under the name and provider number of the clinician performing the services, with explicit exceptions. Commercial payers make their own rules regarding payment policy. They may or may not adopt Medicare's rules, and often they do not. Query each payer regarding its policy on this matter. Get the policy in writing. If a commercial payer declines to provide its policy in writing or simply does not respond to a request, see Recommendation, below.

Recommendation

When a payer does not specifically state that a nurse practitioner's services may be billed under a physician's name or number, a practice is at some risk for a charge of fraud if a payer later claims it wanted services billed under the name and provider number of the individual who actually performed the service. To be very sure that Blue Cross, Aetna, or another payer does not contend, at a later date, that it wanted Medicare's rules followed, the author recommends this strategy:

1. Develop a policy regarding how the practice or facility will bill the nurse practitioner's services, and notify the payers of the policy. For example, the policy might state:

   "Physician services at [insert your practice or facility name here] may be provided by qualified nurse practitioners, under the provisions of state law. Health plans or indemnity insurers who have specific requirements regarding the clinician under whose name such services are billed must state those requirements, in writing, to [insert your practice name here]'s Billing Manager. Lacking written direction from a payer, our

Billing Manager will decide whether a nurse practitioner's services are billed under the nurse practitioner's name or under the name of a physician credentialed with the payer."

2. Mail, certified, the practice's policy to the appropriate contact person at each commercial payer, with a cover letter which states "This is our practice's policy. If your organization has specific requirements regarding billing of physician services provided by nurse practitioners, please respond to me, in writing, specifying such requirements, within 15 days. If I do not receive specific written directions from your organization by [insert date], [insert your practice name here] will assume that this distinction is not important to your organization, and will bill a nurse practitioner's services under one of our physician's names or under the nurse practitioner's name, depending upon which clinician is on the payer's panel.

3. Track and file the payers' responses, and bill accordingly. If there is no response, follow the policy as you have stated it to the payer.

Such a policy, disseminated to each payer, should be sufficient to protect the practice from claims of inappropriate billing. Here is why: Fraud is defined as: "An intentional deception or misrepresentation which the individual knows to be false or does not believe to be true, and the individual is aware that the deception could result in some unauthorized benefit to him/herself or some other person." The practice, if using this strategy, is attempting to correctly represent the services being provided, and there would be no deception or misrepresentation.

How do I get a provider number and/or get credentialed?

The process depends on the payer.

Medicare

Nurse practitioners, like physicians, apply for Medicare provider status by filling out and submitting a CMS 855I form. While awaiting action on the nurse practitioner's provider application, the practice should hold bills until the provider number arrives, then fill in the number and submit.

Medicaid

Nurse practitioners, like physicians, apply for a Medicaid provider number through the state agency which administers Medicaid.

Commercial managed care organizations

Each managed care organization makes its own rules regarding who it will credential and the credentialing and reimbursement process. A practice, institution or facility must query each organization about its policies and respond according to the organization's process.

Commercial indemnity insurers

Each commercial indemnity insurer makes its own rules regarding who it will credential and the process of reimbursement. A practice, institution or facility must query each insurer about its policies and respond according to the organization's process. If the practice, facility or institution already has a contract with an insurer, review the contract to see whether it addresses reimbursement when a nurse practitioner performs a physician service.

Do physicians need to cosign nurse practitioners' orders or progress notes?

No, with exceptions. A state may require a collaborating medical doctor to review a selection of a nurse practitioner's medical record entries. A commercial insurer or managed care organization may make its own rules, and it is possible that a company's rules would include such a requirement. A facility or practice may make its own policies, which may include a requirement that a medical doctor cosign a nurse practitioner's documentation. Such a requirement would be of no value in getting reimbursement, however. And, such a requirement is inadvisable from a malpractice standpoint from the physician's point of view, because the signature may imply more involvement in the medical decision-making on the part of the physician than actually occurred. Neither Medicare nor Medicaid has such a requirement.

CHAPTER 2

BILLING PHYSICIAN SERVICES PERFORMED BY NURSE PRACTITIONERS IN OFFICES

General rules

Each payer makes its own rules. For more on Medicare and Medicaid's rules, and the policies of commercial payers, see Chapter 1. Medicare's rules are the most explicit. The laws and guidelines applicable to physicians billing Medicare apply to nurse practitioners, namely:

- the services must be medically necessary
- the services must be covered by Medicare
- the services must have been provided as billed, and documented in the medical record in a way that justifies the bill
- the clinician must have a Medicare provider number
- the nurse practitioner, employer, or other appropriate entity must submit a claim form—the CMS 1500 form—appropriately completed
- nurse practitioners must accept the payment from Medicare as full payment for the services
- nurse practitioners may not provide or accept kickbacks for referrals and
- payment must be made to the clinician providing the service, in accordance with the rules on reassignment.
Sources: *Medicare Claims Processing Manual*, Chapters 2 and 12, the Federal anti-kickback statutes, and the Center for Medicare and Medicaid Services "Documentation Guidelines for Evaluation and Management Services."

Reassignment

Medicare will pay only certain parties. Under Medicare's rules on reassignment, Medicare will pay the nurse practitioner, the nurse practitioner's employer, an entity to whom the clinician has given the right to payment under a contractual arrangement, an organized health care delivery system if there is a contractual arrangement between the organization and the nurse practitioner, a physician under a locum tenens arrangement, a government agency, or a billing service working under contract with a nurse practitioner. The reassignment rules are provided in the *Medicare Claims Processing Manual*, Chapter 1, Section 30.2.1.

Provider's number on the bill

In general, Medicare requires that services be billed under the provider number of the clinician performing the service. As a general rule, bill nurse practitioner's services under the nurse practitioner's name and/or provider number. There is a difference in the reimbursement Medicare pays to nurse practitioners and physicians. Medicare reimburses services billed under a nurse practitioner's provider number at 85% of 80% of the Medicare Physician Fee Schedule rate. Medicare reimburses physicians at 80% of the Medicare Physician Fee Schedule rate. The patient pays 20% of the Physicians Fee Schedule rate.

Incident-to billing

Under certain circumstances—"incident-to billing—Medicare allows a physician to bill services performed by a nurse practitioner under the physician's provider number. Close attention to the rules is advised, because if a practice inappropriately bills a nurse practitioner's services under a physician's number, the government may demand repayment of the difference between 85% of 80% and 80% of the Physicians Fee Schedule rate, with fines and interest and may mandate compliance activities. If a nurse practitioner's services are billed appropriately under a physician's provider number, using the incident-to rules, Medicare will pay the practice 80% of Medicare's Physician's Fee Schedule rate as compared with 85% of 80% of the Physicians Fee Schedule Rate if services are billed under a nurse practitioner's provider number.

The rules on incident-to billing are found in the *Medicare Benefit Policy Manual*, Chapter 15, Sections 60.1 to 60.3.

The rules for billing a nurse practitioner's services incident-to a physician's services are:

1. The services must be an integral, although incidental, part of the physician's professional service.

2. The services must be commonly rendered without charge or included in the physician's bill.

3. The services must be of a type commonly furnished in physician's offices or clinics.

4. The services must be furnished under the physician's direct personal supervision. Direct supervision does not require the physician's presence in the same examination room but the physician must be present in the same office suite and immediately available.

5. Incident-to billing is not an option when services are performed in a hospital or nursing facility, unless a physician has an office in the nursing facility.

6. When services are performed in the patient's home, incident-to billing is an option only when both the physician and nurse practitioner are present in the patient's home at the time services were performed.

7. The services must be furnished by an individual who is an employee, leased employee or independent contractor of the physician or the practice which employs or contracts with both physician and nurse practitioner.

8. The physician must perform "the initial service and subsequent services of a frequency which reflect his or her active participation in the management of the course of treatment." There is no clarification, to date, regarding the definition of "initial service" or "subsequent services which reflect his or her active participation." See further discussion of this issue, below, under "Example."

9. The physician or other provider under whose name and number the bill is submitted must be the individual present in the office suite when the service is provided.

10. The service must be one which would be covered if furnished by the physician. Source: 42 CFR §410.26.

Example

A physician who employs a nurse practitioner evaluates a patient, and diagnoses hypertension. The physician initiates treatment. The nurse practitioner conducts follow-up visits with the patient, monitoring and treating the hypertension over weeks, months or years. The physician sees the patient every third visit, under a policy adopted by the practice. The nurse practitioner's services (the follow-up visits) may be billed under the physician's provider number, and the practice will receive Medicare's Physicians Fee Schedule rate (Medicare payment plus patient co-pay amount) for the services performed by the nurse practitioner.

However, if the hypertensive patient arrives for a visit with the nurse practitioner, and announces a new complaint—sinusitis, for example—it is not clear that incident-to billing is appropriate. Among auditors and clinicians, there are differing interpretations of the phrase "the physician must perform an initial service," found in the "incident-to" rules. CMS has not defined "initial service." Many clinicians interpret this rule to mean that the first visit to the practice must be conducted by the physician. However, auditors for Medicare interpret "perform an initial service" to mean that when there is a new problem, the nurse practitioner must make a choice—bill under his or her own number or send the patient to the physician for an initial service for the new complaint.

CMS has not elaborated on the phrase "subsequent services of a frequency which reflect his/her active participation in and management of the course of treatment." Therefore, it is unlikely that prosecutors could make a case that a physician did not see a patient often enough to engage in incident-to billing. "Active participation" may mean different things to different clinicians, auditors and administrators. For example, active participation may mean chart review, care oversight, or periodic face-to-face visits, depending upon the reader's interpretation. If active participation means periodic visits, CMS has not provided guidance as to the frequency of physician visits which would indicate "active participation."

Auditors or prosecutors could make a case that incident-to rules were not followed if a practice billed a CPT code for a new patient visit under a physician's provider number and supported

the bill with a progress note written by a nurse practitioner. Furthermore, prosecutors could prove that the incident-to rules were not followed if a practice billed a visit under a physician's provider number, supported the bill with a progress note written by a nurse practitioner and could not establish that the physician was in the suite at the time of the visit.

Billing a non-nurse practitioner's services under a nurse practitioner's provider number

A nurse practitioner or medical practice may bill the services of a non-nurse practitioner incident to a nurse practitioner's services if the rules for incident-to billing are followed. For example, a visit with a registered nurse could be billed with the CPT code for a Level 1 visit under a nurse practitioner's provider number, if incident-to rules are followed. The rules, in that example, would be:

1. The services must be an integral, although incidental, part of the nurse practitioner's professional service.
2. The services must be commonly rendered without charge or included in the physician's bill.
3. The services must be of a type commonly furnished in physician's offices or clinics.
4. The services must be furnished under the nurse practitioner's direct personal supervision. Direct supervision does not require the nurse practitioner's presence in the same examination room but the nurse practitioner must be present in the same office suite and immediately available.
5. Incident-to billing is not an option when services are performed in a hospital or nursing facility.
6. When services are performed in the patient's home, incident-to billing is an option only when both the nurse practitioner and non-

nurse practitioner are present in the patient's home at the time services were performed.

7. The services must be furnished by an individual who is an employee, leased employee or independent contractor of the nurse practitioner or the practice which employs or contracts with both nurse practitioner and non-nurse practitioner.

8. The nurse practitioner must perform "the initial service and subsequent services of a frequency which reflect his or her active participation in the management of the course of treatment."

9. The nurse practitioner under whose name and number the bill is submitted must be the nurse practitioner present in the office suite when the service is provided.

10. The service must be one which would be covered if furnished by the physician.

Example: A patient who initially has seen a nurse practitioner comes to the office for a follow-up blood pressure check. A registered nurse takes the patient's blood pressure. The visit is billed as a Level 1 established patient office visit under the nurse practitioner's provider number.

Recommended practice policies

A practice should adopt one of the following policies:

Policy A: "Bill all visits conducted by a nurse practitioner under the nurse practitioner's provider number." (The practice will get a reduced rate from Medicare, but will not need to have a physician on site or make adjustments if an established patient has a new problem.)

Policy B: "Bill nurse practitioner's visits under either the nurse practitioner or a physician's number, depending upon whether the incident-to rules can be met." If adopting this policy, disseminate information to staff about appropriate incident-to billing. Develop practice policies incorporating the incident-to rules. An example of such a policy is:

For new patients, adopt this policy

"For a patient new to the practice, the receptionist will schedule the first visit with a physician. The physician will perform the entire service and the practice will bill the visit under the physician's provider number. If a physician is unavailable, the receptionist will schedule the patient with a nurse practitioner. In that case, the nurse practitioner will perform the entire service and the practice will bill the visit under the nurse practitioner's provider number."

For established patients, adopt this policy

"Established patients may be scheduled with either a nurse practitioner or physician. If the patient is scheduled with a nurse practitioner, the visit will be billed under the physician's provider number only if the following conditions are met:

a. The physician was in the suite at the time the nurse practitioner saw the patient.

b. The physician saw the patient initially.

c. The physician sees the patient once a year. [Or choose another time frame which reflects the physician's active participation in the management of the course of treatment.]"

For an established patient with a new problem

For an established patient with a new problem, the scenario is likely to be something like this:

Visit 1: Patient Z, a new patient covered by traditional Medicare, is evaluated by Dr. X in July 2003 and diagnosed with chronic sinusitis. Dr. X bills a Level 3 office visit to Part B under Dr. X's provider number. The Physicians Fee Schedule rate is applicable.

Visit 2: In October 2003, Patient Z is evaluated in follow-up of chronic sinusitis by NP Y, an employee of Dr. X. Dr. X was in the suite seeing other patients when the NP conducted the visit, but does not see the patient. NP Y codes a Level 3 office visit, and Dr. X bills the visit under his provider number. The Physicians Fee Schedule rate is applicable.

Visit 3: In January 2004, Patient Z arrives to see the nurse practitioner for follow-up of chronic sinusitis. Patient Z states "I have another problem. I have a lesion on my tongue." The nurse practitioner evaluates and manages both problems, performing a detailed history, detailed examination and Level 4 medical decision-making. Dr. X is in the suite, but does not see the patient.

The dilemma is: Whose provider number may Visit 3 be billed under—Dr. X's or NP Y's? Would the appropriate CPT code (assuming all other requirements are met) be a Level 4 office visit for an established patient, billed under Dr. X, a Level 4 billed under NP Y or a lower level visit billed under Dr. X? The monetary difference between a Level 4 office visit billed under an NP's provider number (85% of the Physicians Fee Schedule rate applies) and a physician's provider number (the Physicians Fee Schedule rate applies) is approximately $12 or more, depending upon the specialty, location of the practice and year the visit is conducted.

Billing a Level 4 office visit under the nurse practitioner's provider number clearly is permissible if the medical record documentation supports that CPT code. Medicare regulations provide no clear answer to the question of whether the practice could bill a Level 4 visit under Dr. X's number, because Dr. X initiated the initial course of treatment for sinusitis but not for the tongue lesion, and the level of service billed is based on both evaluations. However, in recent years Medicare auditors have asserted that a physician must provide the intial service for a new problem, when billing incident-to. So, the NP could send the patient to the physician for evaluation of the tongue lesion.

If the nurse practitioner billed only for the portion of the visit which dealt with the patient's chronic sinusitis (because Dr. X had provided the initial service for the sinusitis), then the visit could be billed appropriately under Dr. X's provider number, but the visit may qualify for only a Level 2 or 3 office visit.

Frequently asked questions regarding incident-to billing

Can an NP bill "incident-to" only in an office setting?

Yes, incident to billing is applicable to office visits only, with two exceptions. The first exception allows incident-to billing when a physician rents office space within a nursing facility and the patient, the NP and the physician are all in that space at the time the NP is rendering service. The second exception is when the NP provides services in the patient's home, and the physician is also in the patient's home.

Can we bill a nurse practitioner's services under a physician's provider number if the nurse practitioner is in a satellite office; i.e. the doctor is not present?

No. In order to bill a nurse practitioner's services incident-to a physician's services, a physician needs to be on site. If a physician is not on site, bill Medicare under the nurse practitioner's provider number.

What about payers other than Medicare? Do they follow the incident-to rules?

The incident-to rules are Medicare's rules, and other payers do not generally follow those rules. Payers other than Medicare—commercial indemnity insurers and managed care organizations—may direct practices to bill an employed nurse practitioner's services under an employer physician's name and/or provider number. Practice managers will need to check each commercial insurer's policy on this matter. If a practice has trouble getting a written response, establish a practice policy and notify the insurer or managed care organization of that policy as recommended below.

Recommendation

When a payer does not specifically state that a nurse practitioner's services may be billed under a physician's name or number, a practice is at some risk for a charge of fraud if a payer later claims it wanted services billed under the name and provider number of the individual who actually performed the service. To be very sure that a payer does not contend, at a later date, that it wanted Medicare's rules followed, the author recommends this strategy:

1. Develop a policy regarding how the practice or facility will bill the nurse practitioner's services, and notify the payers of the policy. For example, the policy might state:

   "Physician services at [insert your practice or facility name here] may be provided by qualified nurse practitioners, under the provisions of state law. Health plans or indemnity insurers who have specific requirements regarding the clinician under whose name such services are billed must state those requirements, in writing, to [insert your practice name here]'s Billing Manager. Lacking written direction from a payer, our Billing Manager will decide whether a nurse practitioner's services are billed under the nurse practitioner's name or under the name of a physician credentialed with the payer."

2. Mail, certified, the practice's policy to the appropriate contact person at each commercial payer, with a cover letter which states "This is our practice's policy. If your organization has specific requirements regarding billing of physician services provided by nurse practitioners, please respond to me, in writing, specifying such requirements, within 15 days. If I do not receive specific written directions from your organization by [insert date], [insert your practice name here] will assume that this distinction is not important to your organization, and will bill a nurse practitioner's services under one of our physician's names or under the nurse practitioner's name, depending upon which clinician is on the payer's panel.

3. Track and file the payers' responses, and bill accordingly. If there is no response, follow the policy as you have stated it to the payer. Such a policy, disseminated to each payer, should be sufficient to protect the practice from claims of inappropriate billing. Here is why: Fraud is defined as: "An intentional

deception or misrepresentation which the individual knows to be false or does not believe to be true, and the individual is aware that the deception could result in some unauthorized benefit to him/herself or some other person." The practice, if using this strategy, is attempting to correctly represent the services being provided, and there would be no deception or misrepresentation.

4. In a satellite office where there is no physician present, bill a nurse practitioner's services under the nurse practitioner's name, unless the practice has a letter, contract or policy from a commercial insurer stating that the nurse practitioner's visits may be billed under a physician's name.

CHAPTER 3

HOSPITAL INPATIENT VISITS[1] AND PROCEDURES

A nurse practitioner may provide physician services to a hospitalized patient if the services are within the scope of practice of a nurse practitioner under state law.

Where state law is silent or unclear, a nurse practitioner may perform procedures specifically delegated by a physician, provided that state law authorizes physicians to delegate their authority to perform medical acts.

When nurse practitioners perform physician services, those services are not included in the prospective payment paid to the hospital by Medicare or other payers for "inpatient hospital services" and may be billed separately. Source: 42 USC 1395x(b) and 42 U.S.C. §1395x (s)(2)(K). And, physician services, whether performed by a physician or nurse practitioner, are not included in the outpatient prospective payment or facility fee, and may be billed separately. Source: 42 CFR 419.22. However, when nurse practitioners perform nursing services in a hospital, those services are covered under the prospective payment to the hospital, and are not billable separately.

Medicare

The rules for billing Medicare for physician services performed by nurse practitioners in hospitals are:

1. Services performed solely by a nurse practitioner must be billed under the nurse practitioner's provider number. There is no opportunity for incident-to billing in the hospital setting. However, there is a way for a team consisting of a nurse practitioner and a physician to bill both the nurse practitioner's and physician's work for a specific patient on a specific day under the physician's provider number and get the full physician fee schedule rate. See "Billing shared visits," page 31.

2. If a nurse practitioner is an employee of a hospital and the nurse practitioner's salary is included in the hospital cost report, and if the hospital receives reimbursement from Medicare Part A under the cost report, then the services of that nurse practitioner may not be billed to Medicare under Part B. Source: Balanced Budget Act of 1997, Social Security Act §1861(s)(K)(i).

---

[1]"Hospital" is defined as "an institution which

(1) is primarily engaged in providing, by or under the supervision of physicians, to inpatients, diagnostic services and therapeutic services for medical diagnosis, treatment, and care of injured, disabled, or sick persons, or rehabilitation services for the rehabilitation of injured, disabled or sick persons; (2) maintains clinical records on all patients; (3) has bylaws in effect with respect to its staff of physicians; (4) has a requirement that every patient with respect to whom payment may be made under this subchapter must be under the care of a physician, except that a patient receiving qualified psychologist services...may be under the care of a clinical psychologist with respect to such services to the extent permitted under State law; (5) provides 24-hour nursing service rendered or supervised by a registered professional nurse, and has a licensed practical nurse or registered professional nurse on duty at all times...; (6) has in effect a hospital utilization review plan which meets the requirements of subsection (k) of this section and has in place a discharge planning process that meets the requirements of subsection (ee) of this section; *[and meets certain licensing and budgetary requirements] Source: 42 U.S.C. §1395x(e)*

3. If the services a nurse practitioner is providing are part of a surgical or maternity package, reimbursed under a global fee, and if a surgeon or obstetrician has billed the global fee, then the nurse practitioner's services may not be billed, as the surgeon or obstetrician already has billed those services. However, there are mechanisms for transferring care and for separating the components of the global fee, which would allow a nurse practitioner's services to be billed. Source: *Medicare Claims Processing Manual*, Chapter 12, 40.1 and 40.2. See "Global fees," below.

4. Nurse practitioners do not have the legal authority to bear sole responsibility for hospitalized patients covered by Medicare, however, even where state law permits. A physician must be involved in the process of care for hospitalized patients covered by Medicare, because, under Federal law governing conditions of participation by hospitals, a hospital's governing body "must ensure that...every Medicare patient is under the care of a doctor of medicine or osteopathy..., a doctor of dental surgery..., a doctor of podiatric medicine..., a doctor of optometry..., a chiropractor,... or a clinical psychologist...." Under Federal law, a doctor of medicine may delegate tasks to other qualified health personnel. Licensed practitioners other than physicians may admit to hospitals if permitted by state law, and if the patient is under the care of a doctor of medicine or osteopathy. Source: 42 CFR 482.12.

Global fees

Medicare reimburses surgeons with a "global fee" which covers a package of surgery-related services defined by a procedure code. If a practitioner other than the surgeon provides some of the services covered by the global fee for a surgery, that practitioner may not get paid. Practitioners need to know which services are covered by the global fee and which services may be billed separately.

The global fee for surgery includes payment for the following services related to the surgery when furnished by the physician who performs the surgery:

- Visits to a patient in an intensive care or critical care unit, if made by the surgeon (however, certain critical care services are payable separately in some situations)

- Preoperative visits, after the decision is made to operate, beginning with the day before the day of surgery for major procedures and the day of surgery for minor procedures

- Intraoperative services that are normally a usual and necessary part of a surgical procedure

- Complications following surgery—all additional medical or surgical services required of the surgeon during the postoperative period of the surgery because of complications

- Postoperative visits during the postoperative period of the surgery that are related to recovery from the surgery

- Post-surgical pain management by the surgeon

- Supplies

- Miscellaneous services, such as dressing changes; local incisional care; removal of operative pack; removal of cutaneous sutures and staples, lines, wires, tubes, drains, casts, and splints; insertion, irrigation and removal of urinary catheters, routine peripheral intravenous lines, nasogastric and rectal tubes; and changes and removal of tracheostomy tubes. Source: *Medicare Claims Processing Manual*, Chapter 12, 40.1.

For the global period for various surgeries, consult *Current Procedural Terminology* and the *Medicare Claims Processing Manual*, Chapter

12, 40.1. For major surgeries, count one day immediately before the day of surgery, the day of surgery and the 90 days immediately following the day of surgery as the global period.

Services not included in the global surgical package; i.e. may be paid separately, include:

- The initial consultation or evaluation of the problem by the surgeon to determine the need for surgery
- Services of other physicians except where the surgeon and the other physician(s) agree on the transfer of care
- Visits unrelated to the diagnosis for which the surgical procedure is performed, unless the visits occur due to complications of the surgery
- Treatment for the underlying condition or an added course of treatment which is not part of normal recovery from surgery
- Diagnostic tests and procedures, including diagnostic radiological procedures
- Clearly distinct surgical procedures during the postoperative period which are not reoperations or treatment for complications
- Treatment for postoperative complications which requires a return trip to the operating room. Source: *Medicare Claims Processing Manual*, Chapter 12, 40.1.

If the surgeon and another physician agree on a transfer of care, then the two physicians submit the procedure code for the surgery with modifiers (-54 or -55). The global fee is split. For example, if a patient travels across the country to a tertiary care hospital for a complicated surgery, then goes home to receive postoperative visits from a local surgeon, the performing surgeon may transfer the care to the local surgeon. The local surgeon will be compensated for his or her services and

the performing surgeon will get a reduced fee. Transfers are subject to anti-kickback scrutiny. For example, Medicare regulations prohibit a referring physician from demanding that a surgeon transfer the patient back to the referring physician for postoperative care and threatening to withhold making referrals to a surgeon who will not agree to split global fees. A transfer of care must be documented in writing. Both the surgeon and the physician providing the postoperative care must keep a copy of the written transfer agreement in the beneficiary's medical record. Source: *Medicare Claims Processing Manual*, Chapter 12, 40.2.

What about minor surgeries and endoscopies?

Visits by the same physician on the same day as a minor surgery or endoscopy are included in the payment for the procedure, unless a significant, separately identifiable service is also performed. The Medicare carriers are instructed to disallow separate payment for postoperative visits or services within 10 days of the surgery that are related to recovery from the procedure.

What if various pre- and postoperative services are covered by practitioners other than the surgeon, but there has been no written transfer of care?

The *Medicare Claims Processing Manual* states that when different physicians in a group practice participate in the care of the patient, the group bills for the entire global package if the physicians reassign benefits to the group. The physician who performs the surgery is shown as the performing physician. Where another physician, not part of the surgeon's group, provides "occasional post-discharge services," but a transfer of care does not occur, the services are reported "by the appropriate evaluation and management code. No modifiers are necessary on the claim." And if the services of a physician other than the surgeon are required during a postoperative period for an underlying condition or medical complication, the other physician reports the appropriate evaluation and management code. No modifiers are necessary. An example is a cardiologist who medically manages the underlying cardiovascular conditions of a patient who has had cardiac surgery.

Are there special considerations when nurse practitioners provide pre- and/or postoperative care?

The *Medicare Claims Processing Manual* does not address a scenario where a nurse practitioner employed by a hospital provides preoperative or postoperative physician services for a patient of a community-based surgeon. And, the manual has no instructions about how to handle the billing of physician services provided by nurse practitioners who work for groups of surgeons. Furthermore, the instructions regarding how to transfer care address physicians, without mention of nurse practitioners or other classes of providers.

The considerations for nurse practitioners are four-fold. First, if a nurse practitioner employed by some entity other than a surgeon is providing services covered by a surgeon's global fee, then the surgeon billing that global fee is billing for services the surgeon has not provided. The surgeon may be billing fraudulently. Second, if a nurse practitioner's employer—a hospital—is paying the nurse practitioner's salary while someone else is billing the nurse practitioner's work, the employer is not only failing to capture revenues, but is subsidizing the surgeon, and that subsidy could be considered a kickback. Third, nurse practitioner services are paid at 85% of the physician's fee schedule rate, so Medicare may be paying 100% of the fee schedule for work reimbursable at 85%. Finally, there is the murky issue of the wording of the Balanced Budget

Act of 1997, which authorized Medicare to pay nurse practitioners directly for physician's services "but only if no facility or other provider charges or is paid any amounts with respect to the furnishing of such services." So, if a hospital which employs a nurse practitioner puts the nurse practitioner's salary in the hospital's cost report, and the hospital receives any cost report-based reimbursement under Medicare, Part A, then Medicare may be paying twice for the same services. Billing Medicare for a service already paid by Medicare is fraud. All of these issues are resolvable. However, surgeons, hospitals and nurse practitioners need to raise the issues so that the Center for Medicare and Medicaid will address them.

Where does one find the rules regarding global fees?

A clinician who reads only *Current Procedural Terminology* (CPT) will be only half-informed regarding the rules, when Medicare or Medicaid is the payer. For example, CPT contains no detailed listing of what is included in the global fee, but simply states "Listed surgical procedures include the operation per se, local infiltration, metacarpal/digital block or topical anesthesia when used, and normal, uncomplicated follow-up care." This explanation falls far short of Medicare requirements, which clearly state that complications of surgery short of a return to the operating room are included in the global fee. Practitioners who perform surgery, or who provide preoperative or postoperative services need to read the periodic transmittals and newsletters from the Medicare Carriers, as well as the *Medicare Claims Processing Manual* section on global fees.

Billing shared visits

There is no opportunity to bill services performed in a hospital under the incident-to rules. However, in 2003 Medicare made a significant change in rules which allow for "shared" billing in situations where a nurse practitioner and a physician employed by the same practice both perform physician services for a hospitalized patient on the same day.

In brief the language says: If a nurse practitioner performs physician services and a physician provides any face-to-face portion of the evaluation/management encounter on an inpatient service, in an outpatient department or in an emergency room, the service may be billed under either the physician's or the nurse practitioner's provider number. However, if there was no face-to-face encounter between the patient and the physician (even if the physician reviewed the medical record) then the service must be billed under the nurse practitioner's provider number. Sources: *Medicare Claims Processing Manual*, Chapter 12, Section 30.6.1.

The manual provides the following guidance:

"**Office/Clinic Setting**—In the office/clinic setting when the physician performs the E/M service, the service must be reported using the physician's UPIN/PIN. When an E/M service is a shared/split encounter between a physician and a non-physician practitioner (NP, PA, CNS or CNM) the service is considered to have been performed "incident-to" if the requirements for "incident-to" are met and the patient is an established patient. If "incident-to" requirements are not met for the shared/split E/M service, the service must be billed under the non-physician practitioner's UPIN/PIN, and payment will be made at the appropriate physician fee schedule payment.

Hospital Inpatient/Outpatient/Emergency Department Setting—When a hospital inpatient/hospital outpatient or emergency department E/M is shared between a physician and a non-physician practitioner from the same group practice and the physician provides any face-to-face portion of the E/M encounter with the patient, the service may be billed under either the physician's or the non-physician practitioner's UPIN/PIN number. However, if there was no face-to-face encounter between the patient and the physician (e.g., even if the physician participated in the service by only reviewing the patient's medical record) then the service may only be billed under the non-physician practitioner's UPIN/PIN. Payment will be made at the appropriate physician fee schedule rate based on the UPIN/PIN entered on the claim.

Examples of shared visits:

1. If the non-physician practitioner sees a hospital inpatient in the morning and the physician follows with a later face-to-face visit with the patient on the same day, the physician or the non-physician practitioner may report the service.

2. In an office setting the non-physician practitioner performs a portion of an E/M encounter and the physician completes the E/M service. If the "incident-to" requirements are met, the physician reports the service. If the "incident-to" requirements are not met, the service must be reported using the non-physician practitioner's UPIN/PIN.

In the rare circumstance when a physician (or non-physician practitioner) provides a service that does not reflect a CPT code description, the service must be reported as an unlisted service with CPT code 99499. A description of the service provided must accompany the claim. The carrier has the discretion to value the service when the service does not meet the full terms of a CPT code description (e.g., only a history is performed). The carrier also determines the payment based on the applicable percentage of the Physician Fee Schedule depending on whether the claim is paid at the physician rate or the non-physician practitioner rate. CPT modifier -52 (reduced services) must not be used with an evaluation and management service. Medicare does not recognize modifier -52 for this purpose."

CMS has adopted a similar approach when two physicians from the same practice see a hospitalized patient on the same day. According to the *Medicare Claims Processing Manual*, Chapter 12, Section 30.6.5.

"If more than one evaluation and management (face-to-face) service is provided on the same day to the same patient by the same physician or more than one physician in the same specialty in the same group, only one evaluation and management service may be reported unless the evaluation and management services are for unrelated problems. Instead of billing separately, the physicians should select a level of service representative of the combined visits and submit the appropriate code for that level."

These rules apply to Medicare only, unless other payers specifically adopt Medicare's rules. There is no law governing commercial payers on this matter.

EXAMPLE of appropriate shared billing: Nurse practitioner visits Patient S in the morning of the patient's second hospital day, and performs a detailed examination and medical decision-making of high complexity. Later that day, a physician in the same practice visits Patient S, and checks the patient's pupillary reaction. The nurse practitioner's and physician's

work is combined and the visit is billed as Level 3 subsequent hospital care, under the physician's provider number.

What not to do

The following billing practices are clearly *inappropriate*, under both the old rules and the new rules, for Medicare patients:

Practice bills a nurse practitioner's evaluation/management service to an emergency room patient under the provider number of a physician employed by the same practice without the physician ever having a face-to-face encounter with the patient.

EXAMPLE: Nurse practitioner evaluates Patient Y in the emergency room and performs a detailed history, detailed examination and medical decision-making of moderate complexity. A physician employed by the same practice is seeing other patients and never lays eyes on the nurse practitioner's patient. Practice bills the CPT code for a Level 4 emergency room visit under the physician's provider number. The practice has billed inappropriately.

Practice bills a nurse practitioner's evaluation/management service to a hospitalized patient under the provider number of a physician employer without the physician having a face-to-face encounter with the patient that day.

EXAMPLE: Nurse practitioner evaluates Patient A in a hospital on day 3 of hospitalization. The nurse practitioner performs all requisites of the CPT code for Level 2 subsequent hospital care. A physician in the practice comes to the floor late that night, reviews the nurse practitioner's note and signs it, noting "Agree," but does not examine or talk with the patient, face-to-face. Practice bills Level 2 subsequent hospital care under the physician's provider number. The practice has billed inappropriately.

What to do

Adopt one of these policies for patients covered by Medicare:

Policy A: Bill any and all visits performed by a nurse practitioner under the nurse practitioner's provider number. If adopting this policy, a physician need not evaluate a patient daily, under Medicare's rules. However, a physician will need to be the "attending physician," who directs the care of the hospitalized patient, to conform with the Federal rules regarding hospitals.

Policy B: Bill a nurse practitioner's services to hospitalized patients under the provider number of a physician in the practice if that physician has seen the patient, face-to-face, that day. The physician must document in the hospital record his/her face-to-face encounter. The CPT code billed may reflect both the nurse practitioner's services and the physician's services.

Commercial payers

As there is no industry standard or applicable law regarding commercial payers, a practice's or hospital's contracts with commercial payers govern the reimbursement process. If a contract says nothing about nurse practitioners and the company will not give a practice or hospital a written policy stating how the company wants nurse practitioner's services billed, see "Recommendation" previous chapter, p. 28.

Recommendation for efficiency, appropriate billing and optimal reimbursement

To make most efficient use of a nurse practitioner's and physician's time while staying within Medicare's rules, have a nurse practitioner perform as much of the evaluation and management service to inpatients as the nurse practitioner can handle, and have a physician in the nurse practitioner's practice see, face-to-face, each patient each hospital day and perform some aspect of the evaluation. The level of physician involvement will be based on the complexity of the patient. Have the nurse practitioner document his or her evaluation in the hospital record, each day. Have the physician document, each day, that he or she has personally performed at least one aspect of the history and/or examination and/or medical decision-making, having evaluated the patient face-to-face. Be sure that each day's documentation answers the question: "Why is this patient hospitalized?" If these conditions have been met, bill the service under the physician's name and provider number. If only the nurse practitioner sees the patient, bill under the nurse practitioner's provider number.

Working plan for a hospital wanting to bill for nurse practitioners' services

Fact-finding for business planning

First, identify the clinical areas where nurse practitioners are practicing. For each nurse practitioner, answer these questions:

1. Are nurse practitioners performing physician services, as defined by:

    a. Code of Federal Regulations, §410.20

    b. *Current Procedural Terminology*, section on Evaluation and Management Services

    c. *Documentation Guidelines for Evaluation and Management*, Center for Medicare and Medicaid Services (CMS).

2. Are nurse practitioners performing administrative or nursing services to such an extent that the nurse practitioners' services which can be billed to third-party payers as physician services is relatively small?

3. Are nurse practitioners' salaries included in the cost report? If so, does the hospital receive any reimbursement under the cost report?

4. What CPT codes would the nurse practitioners use most often?

5. What are the relevant fees attached to these CPT codes?

6. Are the nurse practitioners doing pre-operative and/or post-operative evaluations? If so, are those services covered by the global fee for surgery and/or the anesthesia fees?

7. Are the nurse practitioners employees of the hospital? Are the nurse practitioners leased to any outside entities?

8. Are nurse practitioners employed by the hospital performing services for patients of community physicians (who are not hospital employees)? If so, are the community physicians billing for services the nurse practitioners perform?

9. Are services of nurse practitioners currently being billed under a physician's name/provider number? If so, are rules for shared billing being followed?

Legal research and advice letter

State laws vary regarding scope of practice, qualifications, and physician collaboration requirements for nurse practitioner practice. Federal laws may address specific types of hospital entities, specific specialties and specific procedures. For example, is the entity a hospital, rehabilitation facility, critical access hospital, skilled nursing facility or combination of these entities? The answer may affect how and if a nurse practitioner's services may be billed. Are the treatments the nurse practitioners are providing chemotherapy or end-stage renal disease? Federal rules address each of these treatments. Are the nurse practitioners performing diagnostic testing such as flexible sigmoidoscopy? There is a Federal rule addressing this test.

Each hospital wanting to bill nurse practitioners' services should get an advice letter from an experienced attorney, addressing each of the issues raised above, plus how the hospital must satisfy rules on reassignment and compliance. An advice letter states the facts specific to the organization, the relevant law, the facility's options for billing nurse practitioners' services and the process that must be followed to comply with state and Federal laws.

Business plan

Once the facts are established and the relevant law is identified, the hospital should write a business plan, to include:

a. Service lines
   i. What are they?
   ii. What CPT codes will be most used?
   iii. What is the projected frequency of billings for each frequently-used CPT code?
   iv. How many nurse practitioners work in each service?

b. Payers
   i. Which will reimburse for services provided by NPs?
   ii. Which will reimburse but require bills to be submitted under physician's name?
   iii. Which will reimburse at the best rates?
   iv. What are the usual and customary fees for the CPT codes identified in a.ii. above for each payer?
   v. What is the usual duration between submission of bill and receipt of payment, for each payer?

c. Analysis of payer mix/payment mix

d. Projection of costs related to the billing of nurse practitioner's services (set-up, training, billing, compliance maintenance, contract negotiation, credentialing, evaluation/analysis of payers, payments, and providers)

e. Projection of revenues (previously uncaptured reimbursements and revenues from new service lines)

f. Analysis of current costs/revenue stream compared with costs/revenue stream under new plan

Infrastructure

Tasks

- Obtain provider applications, fill them out, follow-up with payers regarding acceptance
- Set up internal accounting system
- Set up billing system
- Set up compliance plan/program
- Set up policies regarding billing, coding, compliance, documentation, credentialing
- Training

Personnel

To bill nurse practitioners' services, a hospital may require additional personnel, including:

- contract negotiators (payer-provider contracts)
- trainers of nurse practitioners regarding code selection, documenting to support a claim and compliance with Medicare rules
- trainers of billing staff regarding the rules specific to the billing of nurse practitioners' services
- credentialers who would facilitate NPs' provider applications
- account analysts who would periodically evaluate the costs relative to revenues for specific product lines, specific practitioners and specific payers

Policies

To assure efficiency as well as compliance with payer requirements, the hospital should draft and disseminate the following policies:

- qualifications for nurse practitioners who can bill Medicare
- identification of job descriptions under which a nurse practitioners would need a Medicare number
- instructions for completing and processing application, including time-line
- description of circumstances under which services and/and procedures must be billed under the nurse practitioner's number or under a physician's number (shared billing)
- medical necessity, definition and documentation of
- how to select the appropriate CPT code and ICD-9 code for physician services
- compliance plan
- documentation requirements

Periodic analysis/evaluation

Any hospital which initiates a billing program must plan for on-going evaluation, including:

- accounting for each service line
- identification and reward of high-performing clinicians
- retraining of low-performing clinicians
- identification and optimization of high-performing payers
- identification and correction of compliance problems/errors

Training

If a hospital's nurse practitioners are not accustomed to coding their services, they will need training on the basics of billing and coding, coding specific to their specialty area and/or service, compliance requirements and the essentials of hospital and/or practice finance. A hospital's billing staff will need training on the Federal requirements regarding the billing of nurse practitioner's services.

CHAPTER 4

BILLING PHYSICIAN SERVICES PERFORMED BY NURSE PRACTITIONERS IN NURSING FACILITIES

Distinguishing between skilled nursing facilities and nursing facilities

The distinction between skilled nursing facilities and nursing facilities is important for nurse practitioners who practice in these settings. Federal regulations regarding the performance of physician services by nurse practitioners differ, depending on whether the patient is a nursing facility or skilled nursing facility patient.

"Skilled nursing facility" is defined as "an institution (or a distinct part of an institution) which is primarily engaged in providing to residents skilled nursing care and related services for residents who require medical or nursing care or rehabilitation services for the rehabilitation of injured, disabled, or sick persons and is not primarily for the care and treatment of mental diseases...." 42 U.S.C. §1395i-3(a).

''Nursing facility" is defined as "an institution (or a distinct part of an institution) which is primarily engaged in providing to residents, skilled nursing care and related services for residents who require medical or nursing care, rehabilitation services for the rehabilitation of injured, disabled, or sick persons, or, on a regular basis, health-related care and services to individuals who because of their mental or physical condition require care and services (above the level of room and board) which can be made available to them only through institutional facilities, and is not primarily for the care and treatment of mental diseases...." Source: 42 U.S.C. §1396r.

"Skilled nursing facility" is a Medicare term. "Nursing facility" is a Medicaid term.

Physician services and delegation of these services

Federal regulations state:

"A physician must personally approve in writing a recommendation that an individual be admitted to a facility. Each resident must remain under the care of a physician....

[(a) omitted]

(b) Physician visits. The physician must:

(1) Review the resident's total program of care, including medications and treatments, at each visit required by paragraph (c) of this section;

(2) Write, sign and date progress notes at each visit; and

(3) Sign and date all orders.

(c) Frequency of physician visits

(1) The resident must be seen by a physician at least once every 30 days for the first 90 days after admission, and at least once every 60 days thereafter.

(2) A physician visit is considered timely if it occurs not later than 10 days after the date the visit was required.

(3) Except as provided in paragraphs (c) (4) and (f) of this section, all required physician visits must be made by the physician personally.

(4) At the option of the physician, required visits in SNFs after the initial visit may alternate between personal visits by the physician and visits by a physician assistant, nurse practitioner, or clinical nurse specialist in accordance with paragraph (e) of this section.

(d) Availability of physicians for emergency care. The facility must provide or arrange for the provision of physician services 24 hours a day, in case of an emergency.

(e) Physician delegation of tasks in SNFs.

(1) Except as specified in paragraph (e)(2) of this section, a physician may delegate tasks to a physician assistant, nurse practitioner or clinical nurse specialist who

(i) Meets the applicable definition in Sec. 491.2 of this chapter, or, in the case of a clinical nurse specialist, is licensed as such by the State;

(ii) Is acting within the scope of practice as defined by State law; and

(iii) Is under the supervision of the physician.

(2) A physician may not delegate a task when the regulations specify that the physician must perform it personally, or when the delegation is prohibited under State law or by the facility's own policies.

(f) Performance of physician tasks in NFs. At the option of the State, any required physician task in a NF (including tasks which the regulations specify must be performed personally by the physician) may also be satisfied when performed by a nurse practitioner, clinical nurse specialist, or physician assistant who is not an employee of the facility but who is working in collaboration with a physician." Source: 42 CFR §483.40 (b)-(f).

The regulation continues:

"Definitions.

For purposes of this subpart

Facility means, a skilled nursing facility (SNF) or a nursing facility (NF) which meets the requirements of sections 1819 or 1919 (a), (b), (c), and (d) of the Act. "Facility" may include a distinct part of an institution specified in Sec. 440.40 of this chapter, but does not include an institution for the mentally retarded or persons with related conditions described in Sec. 440.150 of this chapter. For Medicare and Medicaid purposes (including eligibility, coverage, certification, and payment), the "facility" is always the entity which participates in the program, whether that entity is comprised of all of, or a distinct part of a larger institution. For Medicare, a SNF (see section 1819(a)(1)), and for Medicaid, a NF (see section 1919(a)(1)) may not be an institution for mental diseases as defined in Sec. 435.1009." Source: 42 C.F.R. §483.5

Recent clarification

On August 16, 2005, the Center for Medicare and Medicaid Services released a "Medlearn Matters" on "Non-Physician Practitioner Questions and Answers." That document is contained in Appendix A of this book.

Certification and recertification of patients

Nurse practitioners may certify and recertify patients for nursing home care, if the nurse practitioner has no direct or indirect employment relationship with the facility and is working in collaboration with a physician. Source: 42 CFR 424.20.

Incident-to billing

When services are provided in a skilled nursing facility or nursing facility, incident-to billing—billing a nurse practitioner's services under a physician's provider number—is permitted only under the following circumstances:

>a. The physician rents office space from the facility.
>
>b. The nurse practitioner, physician and patient all are in that office space at the time the nurse practitioner performs the service.

Unless a. and b. are true, there is no opportunity for incident-to billing of services performed in nursing facilities. Unless services are performed in rented office space within a nursing facility, all services performed by nurse practitioners must be billed under the nurse practitioner's provider number, if the payer is Medicare or Medicaid. The Federal Bureau of Investigation (FBI) has investigated physicians who have billed Medicare under the physician's provider number when services were performed in nursing facilities by nurse practitioners. The FBI gets involved when a Medicare Carrier notices that a physician is billing far more visits per day than he or she could possibly have conducted, and requests an investigation. If, on investigation, the FBI finds that the physician had four nurse practitioners seeing patients, and that the physician billed all of the nurse practitioners' services under the physician's provider number, the next step is a fraud analysis. Fraud is defined as: "an intentional deception or misrepresentation which the individual knows to be false or does not believe to be true, and the individual is aware that the deception could result in some unauthorized benefit to him/herself or some other person." To prove fraud, the government must prove that

the physician knew or should have known the parameters of the incident-to billing rules, but intentionally disregarded the rules, for financial gain. In this set of facts, the financial gain would be the difference between 100% of the Physicians Fee Schedule (if a physician performed the services) and 85% of the Physicians Fee Schedule (if a nurse practitioner performed the services.)

Note that private payers may allow billing of physician services under a nurse practitioner's provider number. Each practice must query each commercial payer regarding the company policy on this matter.

Analysis

Initial comprehensive visit

>*In a skilled nursing facility*: A physician must conduct this visit.
>
>*In a nursing facility*: A nurse practitioner who is not employed by the facility may conduct the visit if state law authorizes a nurse practitioner to do so and if the nurse practitioner is working in collaboration with a physician.

Required visits

>*In skilled nursing facilities*: A nurse practitioner may perform these visits, alternating with a physician, if state law permits. The nurse practitioner may be employed by the facility.
>
>*In nursing facilities*: A nurse practitioner who is employed by the facility may perform these visits, alternating with a physician, if state law permits.

Acute illness/medically necessary visits

In skilled nursing facilities: A nurse practitioner may perform these services, if state law permits. The nurse practitioner may be employed by the facility.

In nursing facilities: A nurse practitioner may perform these services, if state law permits. The nurse practitioner may be employed by the facility.

SUMMARY

Skilled nursing facilities

For a patient in a skilled nursing facility (Medicare is the payer), a nurse practitioner may perform and bill for the following services:

1. Provide required physician visits, except the initial evaluation and readmissions, alternating with a physician, if
    a. the nurse practitioner is acting within the scope of practice as defined by State law,
    b. state law permits physicians to delegate this activity to a nurse practitioner and
    c. the nurse practitioner is collaborating with a physician.
2. Provide medically necessary procedures (visits and other procedures) capable of being described by a CPT code (Current Procedural Terminology) and an ICD-9 code (International Classification of Diseases, 9th revision).
3. Certify and recertify patients for nursing home care.

Nursing facilities

For a patient in a nursing facility (Medicaid is the payer), a nurse practitioner may perform and bill for the following:

1. Provide required physician visits, alternating the required visits with a physician, if:
    a. the nurse practitioner is acting within the scope of practice as defined by State law,
    b. state law permits physicians to delegate this activity to a nurse practitioner and
    c. the nurse practitioner is collaborating with a physician.
2. Provide medically necessary procedures (visits and other procedures) capable of being described by a CPT code (Current Procedural Terminology) and an ICD-9 code (International Classification of Diseases, 9th revision).
3. Certify and recertify patients for nursing home care.

See Appendix B of this book, "CMS Memorandum: Physician Delegation of Tasks."

Frequently asked questions

Initial comprehensive assessment

Q: How do the rules on physician delegation of tasks work in a facility which has both skilled and non-skilled beds?

A: The rules regarding nursing facilities apply to the patients who are admitted to the nursing facility beds and the rules regarding skilled nursing facilities apply to the patients who are admitted to the skilled beds. Sources: 42 CFR 483.5

Q: If a nurse practitioner cannot perform the initial comprehensive assessment on a new patient, but the NP sees the patient before a physician, what heading should the NP put at the beginning of his or her note, i.e. "acceptance note" or "initial assessment"?

A: Use "Acute visit" or "Chronic disease visit" or other descriptor which shows that you are not providing the initial comprehensive evaluation. A nurse practitioner may perform medically necessary visits prior to the initial comprehensive visit.

Q: For patients admitted to non-skilled/long term care beds, private pay, with Blue Cross, can NPs do the initial H&P?

A: You must look at state law and, for Blue Cross, the policy of that company. Federal law authorizes nurse practitioners to perform the initial evaluation for patients in nursing facilities, if state law allows it and the nurse practitioner has a collaborating physician who agrees to it. Source: 42 C.F.R. §483.40.

Recertification

Q: Can NP's recertify for skilled nursing care, if the NP is not employed by the facility?

A: Yes. NPs can certify and recertify for SNF, as long as the NP is not employed by the facility, and as long as state law allows it. Source: 42 C.F.R. §424.20.

Incident-to billing

Q: If the NP is not employed by a nursing facility, and works at a nursing facility, and rents a space within that facility, and the patients are seen in that office, then can the NP bill "incident-to" if the MD is within the same suite during the time the patients are being seen?

A: The rule actually addresses a situation where a physician rents space in the facility. So, the answer is no.

Q: What are the rules for "incident-to" billing in the nursing facility?

A: Incident-to billing is not appropriate for services performed in a nursing or skilled nursing facility, unless a physician rents office space in the facility and that physician, a nurse practitioner and a patient are all in that office space at the time the nurse practitioner performs the services.

CHAPTER 5

PHYSICIAN SERVICES PERFORMED IN PATIENTS' HOMES

Physician vs. nursing services

It is important to keep the distinction between physician services and nursing services clearly in mind, especially when a nurse practitioner provides a house call. Nursing services are reimbursed under a separate payment system from physician services, and a different set of rules apply.

When a nurse practitioner performs medically necessary services (services which would be reimbursed as a physician service if a physician had performed the service, such as evaluating and managing a patient's diabetes), the nurse practitioner's work is billed as a physician visit, using the appropriate procedure and diagnosis codes. The procedure (CPT) codes for home visits are found in *Current Procedural Terminology*. If the payer is Medicare, the service is billed to Medicare Part B; if the payer is Medicaid or a commercial insurer, the visit is billed under the payer's mechanism for billing a physician service. The nurse practitioner does not need a physician's order or referral to perform the visit. The patient need not be confined to the home. Source: *Medicare Claims Processing Manual*, Chapter 12, Section 30.6.14.1. The visit is billed under the nurse practitioner's name and/or provider number.

If a nurse practitioner is providing nursing services (such as assessing the patient's safety at home or providing dressing changes), the nurse practitioner would need a physician's order and certification for home care, the patient would need to meet the definition of "home bound," the visit would need to be conducted through a home care agency which is enrolled as a provider with Medicare and compliant with state requirements for home care agencies, and the bill would be submitted by and paid to the home care agency.

Care plan oversight

Nurse practitioners can perform and bill for care plan oversight, a physician service, reimbursed by Medicare under Part B.

Care plan oversight is a service which recently has been defined as separately reimbursable. Generally, Medicare assumes that physicians oversee the plan of care when certifying and recertifying care and providing medical visits. However, care plan oversight can be billed separately when a physician or nurse practitioner has spent 30 minutes or more per month on the tasks listed below, for an individual patient:

- review of charts, reports, treatment plans, or lab or study results except for the initial interpretation or review of lab or study results that were ordered during or associated with a face-to-face encounter

- telephone calls with other health care professionals (not employed in the same practice) involved in the care of the patient

- team conferences (must document time spent per individual patient)

- telephone or face-to-face discussions with a pharmacist about pharmaceutical therapies
- medical decision-making
- activities to coordinate services (if the coordination activities require the skills of a physician), and
- documenting the service provided.

Services which are **not** countable in the 30 minutes; i.e. time not reimbursed, include:

- time the nurse, nurse practitioner, physician assistant or clinical nurse specialist, or other staff spends getting or filing charts, calling home health aides and patients,
- telephone calls to patient or family, even to adjust medication or treatment
- time spent telephoning prescriptions to the pharmacist
- time spent getting and/or filing the chart, dialing the phone, or time on hold
- travel time
- time spent preparing claims and for claims processing
- initial interpretation or review of lab or study results that were ordered during or associated with a face-to-face encounter
- low intensity services included as part of other evaluation and management services, and
- informal consults with health professionals not involved in the patient's care.

Care plan oversight is billed using the HCPCS code G0181.

Nurse practitioners' authority to bill for care plan oversight comes from the Center for Medicare and Medicaid Services in Transmittal B-00-65 issued November 21, 2000. It stated:

"We are also clarifying that, under the provision of the Balanced Budget Act of 1997, nurse practitioners, physician assistants, and clinical nurse specialists, practicing within the scope of State law, may bill for care plan oversight. These non-physician practitioners must be providing ongoing care for the beneficiary through evaluation and management services (but not if they are involved only in the delivery of the Medicare covered home health or hospice service)."

In spite of the unequivocal statement that Medicare will pay nurse practitioners for care plan oversight, some Medicare carriers reportedly have denied such payments. And, the June 1, 2002 issue of the *Medicare Part B Newsletter*, put out by Trailblazer Health, a Medicare carrier serving Texas, Maryland, the District of Columbia and Virginia, answered a "frequently asked question" as follows:

"Q. Can a physician other than the physician who signed the plan of care (i.e., attending physician) bill for care plan oversight?

A. The physician who bills for care plan oversight must be the same physician who signs the plan of care." Source: *Medicare Part B Newsletter No. 02-026*, June 1, 2002, p. 25.

It is clear that nurse practitioners cannot sign the plan of care. The United States Code (42 U.S.C. §1395n (a)(2)(a)) states that Medicare will pay for home care if a physician certifies (and recertifies, where such services are furnished over a period of time) that the services are or were required because the individual is or was confined to his home, that the patient needs or needed skilled nursing care or physical, speech, or occupational therapy on an intermittent basis, that a plan for furnishing such services has been established and is periodically reviewed by a physician, and that such services are or were furnished while the individual is or was under the care of a physician. CMS Transmittal 302, *Medicare Home Health Agency Manual*, July 26, 2002, p. 14.3, states: "The physician who signs the plan of care must be qualified to sign the certification as described in 42 C.F.R. §424.22." That regulation states: "Medicare Part A or Part B pays for home health services only if a physician certifies and recertifies...that...(i) The individual needs or needed intermittent skilled nursing care..., (ii) Home health services were required because the individual was confined to home, and (iii) A plan for furnishing the services has been established and is periodically reviewed by a physician who is a doctor of medicine, osteopathy or podiatric medicine, and who is not precluded from performing this function under paragraph (d) of this section...." The regulation also requires that recertification be signed by the physician who reviews the plan of care.

In a Final Rule "Medicare Program; Revisions to Payment Policies Under the Physician Fee Schedule for Calendar Year 2002," published November 1, 2000 in the *Federal Register*, p. 65407, CMS reiterated that nurse practitioners cannot certify a patient for home care, stating:

> "Sections 1814(a)(2)(C) and 1835 (a)(2)(A) of the [Social Security] Act require that physicians certify and recertify the necessity of home health care in order for a particular beneficiary to receive covered services. Thus, without regard to payment issues, in order to be effective, a certification must be made by a physician. We agree with commenters that, according to section 1861(s)(2)(K) of the Act, nurse practitioners and others can perform and where appropriate, bill for a service that is a physician service and within the scope of their practice. In adopting codes for certification and recertification of home health services and denominating them as billable physician services, we might be perceived as enabling these practitioners to bill those codes. However, nurse practitioner and others not specified under section 1861(r) of the Act cannot meet the requirements for certifying and recertifying home health services under sections 1814 and 1835 of the Act that independently require physician certification and recertification to establish the necessity of treatment."

So, a nurse practitioner can perform and bill care plan oversight. The rules for billing care plan oversight are found in the *Medicare Claims Processing Manual*, Chapter 12, Section 180.1. However, as noted above, at least one Medicare Carrier thinks care plan oversight must be billed by the physician who signed the plan of care. The problem is that the law on home care, developed many years ago, has not been updated or changed to conform with the Balanced Budget Act of 1997, which authorized Medicare to pay nurse practitioners who perform physician services. Several professional organizations are working on a bill to update the Social Security Act on this matter.

FREQUENTLY ASKED QUESTIONS

Q: Can NPs do home visits and get reimbursed?

A: Yes. Medicare will reimburse NPs, under Part B, for performing medically necessary physician services in a patient's home. Some private third party payers do cover home visits, and some do not, no matter who performs the service.

Confusion arises when payers and clinicians do not understand the distinction between nursing services, which are provided by a nurse who works for a home care agency, and which are reimbursed under Medicare Part A, and physician services provided by a nurse practitioner, which are reimbursed under Medicare Part B.

Q: Are visits to patients in the assisted living homes home visits or are those visits billed under "domiciliary" codes? If so, what are "domiciliary" codes?

A: Visits to the home of individuals who live in assisted living are billed using the CPT codes for domiciliaries.

Use the procedure codes for "Domiciliary, rest home or custodial services" listed in *Current Procedural Terminology* when providing evaluation and management services in a facility which provides room, board and other personal assistance services, generally on a long-term basis. The facility's services generally do not include a medical component.

CHAPTER 6

HOSPICE

Definition of hospice

"Hospice care," "end-of-life care" and "palliative care" are often used interchangeably. However, a hospice is a legally defined provider of end-of-life services, subject to requirements of Federal and state law. End-of-life care and palliative care can be given to a patient whether or not that patient is enrolled in hospice. If a patient enrolled in hospice, Federal and state laws apply. For patients enrolled in hospice, Medicare, Medicaid and some third-party payers will cover:

- Medical care, through the hospice medical director
- Nursing care
- Pharmaceutical therapy for pain relief and symptom control
- Home health aide and homemaker services
- Social work services
- Physical and occupational therapy
- Speech therapy
- Diet counseling
- Bereavement and other counseling services
- Case management

For nurse practitioners, the legal distinction between a patient enrolled in hospice and a patient who is getting palliative care or end-of-life care but is not enrolled in hospice is important, because Federal law requires that a physician—defined as a doctor of medicine or osteopathy—perform certain functions for hospice patients. A physician must determine that a patient has 6 months or less to live. The medical director of hospice must be a physician. The Federal law on hospice says:

"The hospice must obtain written certification of terminal illness.... The certification must specify that the individual's prognosis is for a life expectancy of 6 months or less if the terminal illness runs its normal course.... For the initial 90-day period, the hospice must obtain written certification statements...from (i) The medical director of the hospice or the physician member of the hospice interdisciplinary group; and (ii) The individual's attending physician if the individual has an attending physician. ...For subsequent periods, the only requirement is certification by one of the physicians listed...." Source: 42 C.F.R. §418.22

"The medical director must be a hospice employee who is a doctor of medicine or osteopathy who assumes overall responsibility for the medical component of the hospice's patient care program." Source: 42 C.F.R. §418.54

"When hospice coverage is elected, the beneficiary waives all rights to Medicare Part B payments for services that are related to the treatment and management of his/her terminal illness during any period his/her hospice benefit election is in force, except for professional services of an "attending physician." Source: *Medicare Claims Processing Manual*, Chapter 11, Section 40.1.3.

A recent act of Congress adds nurse practitioners to those who may be attending physicians. The "Medicare Prescription Drug, Improvement, and Modernization Act of 2003" changed §1861(dd)(3)(B) of the Social Security Act (42 U.S.C. §1395x(dd)(3)(b)) to authorize a nurse practitioner to be the attending physician for a patient enrolled in hospice. (A physician still must determine that a patient has six months or less to live.) See Appendix C of this book, "Nurse Practitioner Services Under Medicare Hospice."

For purposes of administering the hospice benefit provisions, an "attending physician" is identified by the individual, at the time he/she elects hospice coverage, as having the most significant role in the determination and delivery of their medical care." Source: *Medicare Claims Processing Manual*, Chapter 11, Section 40.1.3.

Hospice medical director services

Medical services to patients enrolled in hospice may be provided by a hospice medical director or by an attending physician (or attending nurse practitioner) who the patient names at the time the patient elects hospice. For patients covered by Medicare, the following services performed by hospice physicians are included in the payment to the hospice under Part A Medicare:

> (1) General supervisory services of the medical director
>
> (2) Participation in the establishment of plans of care
>
> (3) Supervision of care and services
>
> (4) Periodic review and updating of plans of care and
>
> (5) Establishment of governing policies by the physician member of the interdisciplinary group.

For any other medical service, Medicare will pay hospice 100% of the physician's reasonable charge for those physician services furnished by hospice employees or under arrangements with the hospice. Services furnished voluntarily by physicians are not reimbursable.

Attending physician services

When a Medicare beneficiary elects hospice coverage he/she may designate an attending physician (or nurse practitioner) not employed by the hospice who will care for the patient with the hospice physician. The professional services of a non-hospice affiliated attending physician or nurse practitioner for the treatment and management of a hospice patient's terminal illness are not considered "hospice services." If the patient's attending physician or nurse practitioner is not an employee of the hospice or providing services under arrangements with the hospice, the attending physician or nurse practitioner may bill Medicare Part B for his/her services, using a GV modifier, which indicates "Attending physician not employed or paid under agreement by the patient's hospice provider." Medicare will pay the attending physician 80% of the reasonable charge. The patient will pay 20%. Sources: 42 CFR §418.304, the *Hospice Manual* (Publication 21), §406 and the *Medicare Claims Processing Manual*, Chapter 11, Section 40.1.3.

Physicians who are not hospice medical directors or attending physicians may bill Medicare for services not related to the hospice patient's terminal condition. These services are coded with a GW modifier ("Service not related to the hospice patient's terminal condition"). Carriers will process such services in the normal manner for coverage and payment determination. Source: *Medicare Claims Processing Manual*, Chapter 11, Section 50.

State law also addresses hospice and may require that physicians deliver the services to patients in hospice.

Where to find the rules on hospice

The rules for billing Medicare for hospice services are found in 2 documents: the *Code of Federal Regulations* (42 C.F.R. §418.54, §418.58 and §418.304), the *Medicare Claims Processing Manual*.

For Medicaid's rules, visit the web site of the state Medicaid agency.

Commercial payers each have their own rules on coverage of hospice.

Billing for end-of-life care for patients not in hospice

When a nurse practitioner provides medically necessary physician services to a patient who is at end of life but who is not enrolled in hospice, the nurse practitioner bills the service according the same rules governing services to patients who are in early or mid-life. For example, if treating the nausea or pain of a patient who is terminally ill with cancer, a nurse practitioner might bill Medicare for an office visit, using one of the evaluation and management procedure codes and a diagnosis code for nausea, pain and/or cancer.

For payment, payers require that a service be:

• medically necessary

• a physician service described by a CPT code and an ICD-9 code

• covered under the patient's policy and

• documented in the patient's record.

Additional requirements:

• The service must not have been billed or paid already.

• The provider of services must be credentialed or otherwise acceptable to the payer.

• The provider must follow the rules of the payer regarding claims.

Frequently asked question

Q: Regarding hospice, we have hospice patients in all different practice settings: skilled, long term care, assisted living at home, assisted living in clinic and outpatient. Does setting influence what a nurse practitioner can perform and bill? Are there any billing glitches regarding NP visits with hospice patients in all of the different settings? Can NPs order hospice in any of the settings?

A: NPs cannot order hospice. A patient in any setting can be enrolled in hospice. If a patient names a nurse practitioner as the patient's attending physician, the nurse practitioner can treat the terminal illness and bill for the treatment services.

If an NP is employed by a specialist who is treating a condition other than the terminal illness and if neither the hospice nor the attending physician (or nurse practitioner) is billing for that specialty service, then it is possible that a nurse practitioner could provide the specialist's service and bill Medicare Part B. The specialist would need to communicate with the hospice medical director to ascertain that hospice is not addressing the condition through another specialist.

CHAPTER 7

AVOIDING AUDITS, INVESTIGATIONS AND FRAUD

What is fraud and abuse in billing matters?

Fraud is defined as: "an intentional deception or misrepresentation which the individual knows to be false or does not believe to be true, and the individual is aware that the deception could result in some unauthorized benefit to him/herself or some other person."

Billing abuse is defined as: "payment for items or services when there is no legal entitlement to that payment, and the physician has not knowingly and intentionally misrepresented facts to obtain payment."

False claims are claims which health care providers know or should know will lead to greater payments than are appropriate. A charge of false claims could be made against a clinician who or practice which engages in a pattern or practice of submitting claims for services that the provider knows or should have known are not medically necessary.

Any payer—Medicaid, Medicare or commercial insurers—may investigate and prosecute suspected abuse of its processes. The Federal government has been the most active in detecting and prosecuting fraud and abuse in recent years, in relation to Medicare and Medicaid.

Who investigates fraud?

If a Medicare Carrier suspects that a provider has billed services not rendered, not rendered as billed or not documented as billed, the Carrier may report the provider to the Center for Medicare and Medicaid Services (CMS). CMS may report the provider to the Office of the Inspector General, which will contact the Justice Department, which contacts the FBI, whose agents conduct an investigation. For Medicaid, the investigators are employees of the state Medicaid agency and the state police.

Payers may also respond to complaints from patients, disgruntled employees of practices or facilities, or other individuals who have reason to believe a provider is billing inappropriately. Payers may contract with auditors who may conduct random or targeted evaluations of a provider's documentation, whether or not the Carrier, a patient or another individual has filed a complaint.

Who makes the rules?

For Medicare, CMS drafts the rules and conducts the process of review and finalization of rules and regulations. CMS oversees Medicare carriers—the regional contractors which actually pay bills. Medicare Carriers are private contractors who pay, on behalf of CMS, the claims submitted by health care providers. Carriers follow directions given by CMS; specifically the *Medicare Manuals* and related transmittals. CMS must follow Federal statutes, but may write rules and regulations which provide detail not covered by a statute.

For Medicaid, the state Medicaid agency makes the rules, based on laws passed by state legislatures.

For commercial insurers and managed care organizations, the company itself makes the rules, but must abide by any state or federal law applicable to the insurer or organization.

What kind of errors may be considered fraud?

Irregularities which can lead to a fraud investigation include:

1) Submitting high-level procedure codes for diagnoses which do not warrant a high-level evaluation,

2) Submitting high-level procedure codes but failing to document a level of work which supports the bill,

3) Submitting procedure codes which form patterns which fall out of the expected patterns of billing, and

4) Billing separately for services which, according to the rules, should be billed together (bundled). An example is billing separately for the components of a diagnostic chemistry panel to increase reimbursement, when the tests should have been billed under the code for a chemistry panel.

Irregularities 1-3 are "upcoding." Irregularity 4 is "unbundling." Upcoding, unbundling and billing for unnecessary services are three areas which the government has identified as problem areas. Auditors will be looking for claims which:

• Misrepresent the actual provider
• Misrepresent the service provided
• Misrepresent the diagnosis

Example: Misrepresenting the provider

A physician employed four nurse practitioners. He billed all procedures performed by the nurse practitioners under his own Medicare provider number, regardless of whether the "incident-to" rules were followed. He was investigated. He settled with the Federal government to repay $40,000, pay for audits of his billings, attend training and pay fines.

Example: Misrepresenting the service provided

A physician billed millions of dollars to Medicare for office visits for patients for whom no documentation was found, for patients who were deceased and for patients who did not exist. The physician was found guilty of Medicare fraud.

Example: Misrepresenting the diagnosis

A hospital was investigated and ordered to repay $4.5 million in payments for thousands of discharges for complicated pneumonia. The hospital's documentation supported only simple pneumonia, which brings a smaller payment than complicated pneumonia. The case against the hospital was built on a comparison of the hospital's data and aggregate data from other hospitals. The hospital's cases billed as complex pneumonia rose to 79% of all pneumonias in 1994 from 38% in 1993, sending off a red flag to investigators. Nationally, hospitals were billing for the rare strain at a 3-4% rate.

Waiver of copayments is considered fraud

Waiving copayments may be billing abuse or fraud, according to the Federal government. Waiving copayments encourages overutilization by patients. Furthermore, physician payments are based, among other things, on assertions by physicians that a visit is worth at least the amount stated in the physicians fee schedule. If health care providers are willing to provide the services for 20% less than expected, then the physicians' fee schedule is based on fraudulent information. Furthermore, waiver of copayments may violate the anti-referral laws, in that the provider is offering the patient a financial incentive—a kickback—for coming to the provider's practice; that is, patients are more likely to go to a provider who waives the copayment.

In specific cases of patients' financial hardship, a health care provider may waive copayments and write off balances due. However, this should not be done routinely, and the write-offs should be noted in the patient's medical record. The health care providers should also document attempts to collect copayments.

What kinds of activities may be considered billing abuse?

Because Federal enforcement efforts have focused on hospitals in recent years there are abundant examples of charges of abuse by hospitals.

Hospital example #1

A hospital misused the billing code for global prenatal care. Under the rules, to obtain a reimbursement of $550 for prenatal care, the same physician, nurse practitioner or physician assistant had to provide five or more prenatal visits. If a different clinician provided each visit, the reimbursement was $17 per visit. The hospital submitted bills under the code for global prenatal care when various physicians, nurses, nurse practitioners and medical students had performed the services. The hospital was ordered to repay payments made and to pay high fines as a penalty.

Hospital example #2

A hospital billed Medicaid for deliveries by physicians when medical students, nurses or other health care providers who were not enrolled in the Medicaid program performed the deliveries. A physician signed the medical record long after the delivery.

Hospital example #3

An academic medical center billed for the services of attending physicians when there was insufficient documentation to show that the physicians were personally involved.

Hospital example #4

A hospital billed Medicare for hospital admissions. A Medicare audit determined that the care could have been provided on an outpatient basis.

Hospital example #5

A hospital paid kickbacks to physicians in exchange for referrals. Kickbacks were in the form of investment opportunities in the hospital or medical directorships, where the value of the investment, or the salary for the job, was directly related to the number of referrals. Other kickbacks included free rent for doctors, recruiting services, hunting and fishing trips and other travel.

What can happen to a physician, nurse practitioner or facility charged with health care fraud?

Among the charges which the government, or a private insurer, could bring are health care fraud, embezzlement of health care funds, false statements relating to health care, obstruction of justice, and money laundering. The most common charge against health care providers is health care fraud.

Possible penalties against a health care provider who commits fraud could include:

- Fines
- Permanent exclusion from the Medicare program
- Loss of ability to enter into Medicare agreements
- Exclusion of an entity controlled by a family member of a sanctioned individual

- Civil money penalties for individuals who contract with an excluded individual
- Incarceration
- Mandated training, auditing, reporting and record-keeping
- Loss of license.

The government orders health care providers to repay money paid in error. Documentation errors or omissions short of fraud can lead to denial of payments or demands for repayment of monies already paid a provider.

What about honest mistakes?

Auditors and investigators will consider the following factors in determining whether mistakes are "honest mistakes":

- Were the mistakes always in favor of the provider?
- What would an objective observer think about these mistakes? Do they arouse suspicion in the impartial observer?
- Could the mistake have resulted from a reasonable differing interpretation of the rules?

Common errors which health care providers have claimed are good faith errors include:

- Reporting improper diagnosis or procedure codes
- Billing twice for the same service
- Billing for services not covered by the patient's policy (such as billing a routine physical exam, which is not covered by Medicare)
- Providing no documentation for the medical necessity of provided services, and
- Misrepresenting information (such as representing a routine physical examination as a disease-related encounter).

How does the government find out about these errors?

There are at least three sources of information about a practice's or facility's billing practices:

- Complaints by an employee or former employee of a medical practice or facility
- Complaint from a patient
- Identification of irregularities through prepayment or postpayment reviews conducted by Medicare carriers.

A compliance plan for practices

The Federal government expects medical practices, even individual and small group practices, to set up internal auditing systems and conduct periodic self-audits to ascertain that billing is being done correctly. If bills have incorrectly represented the work documented, and the government has overpaid a practice or facility, the government wants the money back.

The Office of the Inspector General (OIG) made its expectations clear in an 18-page notice— "OIG Compliance Program for Individual and Small Group Practices—published in the *Federal Register* on October 5, 2000.

Compliance programs are voluntary, unless mandated after a failed audit. Compliance programs are good for business, says the OIG, because they speed and optimize proper payment of claims, minimize billing mistakes, and reduce the chances that an audit will be conducted by the Carrier or OIG. Self-audits also demonstrate that a practice is making good faith efforts to submit claims appropriately, says the OIG. An effective compliance program, says the OIG, involves seven steps:

1. Conducting internal monitoring and auditing;
2. Implementing compliance and practice standards;

3. Designating a compliance officer or contact;

4. Conducting appropriate training and education;

5. Responding appropriately to detected offenses and developing corrective action;

6. Developing open lines of communication and

7. Enforcing disciplinary standards through well-publicized guidelines.

Internal monitoring and auditing

Step 1 calls for practices to initiate and continue, at regular intervals, two types of self-audits—a standards audit and a claims submission audit. A standards audit determines whether the practice has up-to-date policies, standards, and procedures. A claims submission audit reviews a sample of bills and medical records—5 to 10 per physician—to determine whether the correct procedure and diagnosis codes were used, whether the record supports the visit as billed, whether medical necessary is documented in the record and whether any incentives for unnecessary services exist.

Implementing compliance

Step 2 calls for practices to develop procedures for attending to the areas of risk identified in Step 1. That is, if a self-audit revealed that a physician or nurse practitioner is coding higher or lower than is supported by their medical record notes, Step 2 would require a practice to set up a program or procedures whereby that deficiency would be corrected.

What is required if mistakes are uncovered?

Practices which have billed inappropriately need to pay back the money they have been overpaid, says the OIG.

Step 5 of a compliance plan calls for "responding appropriately to detected offenses and

developing corrective action." If, after setting up its own rules for monitoring for errors, a practice detects errors, the practice must determine whether a significant violation of law has occurred. If so, the practice must take decisive steps to correct the problem. Such steps should involve changing procedures to assure that the problem does not recur, but also returning any overpayments the practice has received.

The OIG expects practices to pay attention to the following "warning indicators":

- significant changes in the number and/or types of claim rejections and/or reductions

- correspondence from the carriers and insurers challenging the medical necessity or validity of claims

- illogical patterns or unusual changes in the pattern of CPT or ICD-9 code utilization, and

- high volumes of unusual charge or payment adjustment transactions.

For example, Medicare Carriers expect that a practice's bills for evaluation and management visits, Levels 1 to 5, will fall in a bell curve, with Level 3 visits occurring most frequently. If a practice's compliance officer notes that bills are skewed towards Levels 4 and 5, the compliance officer should arrange an audit of notes for the higher level visits, to determine whether the documentation supports the level of visit billed. If so, the practice, if audited, will have evidence to prove that the higher level billings were justified, possibly because the practice's patients are more complex than average. If documentation does not support the bills, the practice should initiate interventions, such as repaying monies overpaid by the government or other insurers and training of clinicians about proper coding and documentation.

"For potential criminal violations, a physician

practice would be well advised in its compliance program procedures to include steps for prompt referral or disclosure to an appropriate Government authority or law enforcement agency. In regard to overpayment issues, it is advised that the physician practice take appropriate corrective action, including prompt identification and repayment of any overpayment to the affected payer," says the OIG.

Are nurse practitioner practices expected to have compliance programs?

The OIG's compliance program guidance is intended to assist "physician" practices. The OIG's definition of "physician" does not include nurse practitioners. However, the OIG states "Much of this guidance can also apply to other independent practitioners, such as psychologists, physical therapists, speech language pathologists, and occupational therapists." Physician practices which employ nurse practitioners should include nurse practitioners in training on coding and billing and should conduct audits on nurse practitioner's notes.

What does self-disclosure get a practice?

Here is what the Inspector General has said about the Provider Self-Disclosure Protocol: "While voluntary disclosure under the protocol does not guarantee a provider protection from civil, criminal or administrative actions, the fact that a provider voluntarily disclosed possible wrongdoing is a mitigating factor in OIG's recommendations to prosecuting agencies." Self-reporting offers providers the opportunity to minimize the potential cost and disruption of a full-scale audit and investigation, to negotiate a fair monetary settlement, and to avoid an OIG permissive exclusion preventing the provider from doing business with Federal health care programs.

When to consult an attorney

The OIG itself suggests that physicians consult an attorney before self-disclosing errors and/or overpayments to the OIG. Attorneys are bound by their code of professional conduct to keep all client disclosures confidential. Attorney work product is protected from subpoena. Physician practices which discover errors that resulted in overpayments should initiate an attorney-client relationship with an attorney experienced in these matters.

CHAPTER 8

OPTIMIZING REIMBURSEMENT BY AVOIDING DENIALS

Some practices are reporting that their percentage of claims uncollected 60 days after submission is rising. Slow payment may be a business strategy of a commercial insurer or health plan. In some states, legislatures are attempting to remedy that problem by enacting "prompt pay" laws. Sometimes, payments may be slow in coming, or denied, because the practice or facility did not complete all of the necessary steps to submit a clean claim. A clean claim is a billing form which has all of the necessary blanks filled in, and answers which conform to the insurer's requirements. Here is a checklist for determining whether a practice has completed all of the steps necessary for getting paid:

For Medicare, have you:

- Applied for and received a provider number for the site from which you are submitting the bill? (If billing "incident-to" has the physician received a provider number for the site where the services were rendered?)
- Ascertained that the incident-to rules have been followed, if billing incident-to?
- Ascertained and documented that the service is medically necessary
- Submitted an appropriate CPT and ICD code?
- Made sure that you have chosen an ICD code that indicates that the service is medically necessary? (*Example:* EKG is not a medically necessary service if only one ICD code is submitted and it is for "dysuria.")
- Provided all of the ICD codes applicable to the patient, including chronic illnesses which may have factored into the decision to order diagnostic tests or referrals that day?
- Ascertained that the ICD code you provided has 5 digits (unless the appropriate ICD code is one where only 3 or 4 digits are required)?
- Determined that the service is covered by Medicare?
- Made sure that your lab is registered with the appropriate state agency or that you have a waiver? If you have a waiver, the billed test must be one that is on the list of waived tests.
- Ascertained that the patient is covered by Medicare?
- Ascertained that your state law authorizes a nurse practitioner to perform the service you are billing, if a nurse practitioner has performed the service?
- Added a modifier -25 to the CPT code for the evaluation, if another procedure and an evaluation are provided that day?
- Ascertained that the service has not been billed already?

For Medicaid, have you:

- Applied for and received a provider number?
- Submitted an appropriate CPT and ICD code?
- Determined that the patient's coverage is current as of the date of service?

- Determined that the service is covered by Medicaid?

- If billing for a lab test, made sure that your lab conforms to any state Medicaid requirements for billing that test?

- Determined whether the patient is covered by a Medicaid managed care plan? If the patient is covered by a managed care plan, see "For patients covered by a managed care plan," below.

For commercial indemnity insurers, have you:

- Been approved as a preferred provider, if the insurer requires such designation?

- Been assigned a provider number with the insurer, if the insurer requires it?

- Been credentialed with the insurer, if so required?

- Submitted a CMS 1500 to the insurer, with a CPT and ICD code which appropriately describes the services provided?

- Provided services which are medically necessary (or preventive services covered under the policy) and not excluded by the terms of the policy?

- Used a laboratory approved by the insurer?

- Ascertained that the patient's coverage is current?

For patients enrolled in a managed care plan (HMO or MCO) have you:

- Applied for and received approval as a network provider?

- Received approval from the patient's Primary Care Provider to provide the services (unless you are the patient's PCP)?

- Determined that the service is covered under the patient's plan?

- Read and understood your contract with the company?

- Adhered to the terms of the contract between you or the practice and the managed care plan?

- Determined that the service you are billing is not included in a capitated fee?

- Submitted the bill on the form the company requires for such billings?

- If the service is a diagnostic test provided in-office, have you determined that your contract allows you to bill for the service?

- Determined that the patient's coverage is current?

- Gathered and read all contracts between the practice and insurers or managed care plans, looking specifically for any requirements regarding billing of nurse practitioner services, services excluded from coverage and requirements for prior approval; for example, from a Primary Care Provider or utilization manager?

- Periodically analyzed the various companies regarding how promptly they pay claims and how frequently they deny claims?

15 Documentation "Do's"

1. If billing Medicare "incident-to" a physician's service—billing NP services in office under a physician's number to get 100% of the physicians' fee schedule amount—a physician must conduct and document the initial visit; i.e., there should be no notes written by a NP for initial visits billed under a physician's Medicare number.

2. If billing under the NP's own Medicare number (which will bring 85% of the physician's fee schedule amount for the CPT code billed), the NP should conduct and document all visits, performed in any setting, unless the NP and his or her assistant are working in an office and have followed the "incident-to" rules.

3. Always document a clinical impression or diagnosis in the progress note. When the clinician has not determined the patient's diagnosis, document symptoms, physical findings, differential diagnoses or "rule out" diagnoses. However, claim forms must include ICD-9 codes, and there are no ICD-9 codes for "rule outs." If the diagnosis is in the rule-out stage, select the ICD-9 code for a symptom. Example: Patient has dysuria, but UTI has not been confirmed. Write either "dysuria" or "rule out UTI" as the diagnosis in the progress note, and bill the ICD-9 code for "dysuria."

4. For a problem with an established diagnosis, note whether the problem is improved, well-controlled, resolving, resolved or inadequately controlled, worsening, or failing to change as expected.

5. Document the initiation of or changes in treatment, patient instruction, therapies and medications. All of these efforts will be considered by auditors when they are validating the level of visit billed.

6. If referrals are made, make it clear, in the record and on the referral form, that the referral is "for consultation" or "for evaluation and management."

7. Document review of diagnostic tests. "Chest x-ray normal" is acceptable, or, the review may be documented by dating and initialing the document containing the test result.

8. If a clinician reviews an EKG with a cardiologist in a face-to-face consultation, write "reviewed EKG with Cardiologist X." Consultation with other providers raises the level of medical decision-making, and therefore raises the level of code billed.

9. Document comorbidities, underlying diseases or other factors which increase the complexity of the medical decision-making by increasing the risk of complications, morbidity and/or mortality.

10. If a clinician spends more than 50% of the face-to-face time counseling a patient, the clinician may elect to bill the level of service based on counseling and/or coordination of care. Use an evaluation and management procedure code, based on the total length of time of the face-to-face encounter. Use the times given in *Current Procedural Terminology* (CPT) for each level of visit. Record the time the visit started and ended and describe the counseling. The note may be brief. Counseling may include discussion about diagnostic test results, prognosis, treatment options, instructions for treatment, importance of compliance, reduction of risk factors, and patient and family education. (Note that counseling is not psychotherapy, which is billed under different codes and different rules.) If the practice uses patient instruction sheets, reference the sheet by name or number.

11. If deferring a specific element of an examination, document the reason for deferral.

12. Write each note so that it can stand alone to justify the bill. Auditors usually ask for documentation of a visit on a particular day. Clerks responding to such requests usually include only the record for the day requested. Generally, auditors will not request previous notes or problem lists to answer any questions they may have.

13. Every day of a patient's hospital stay, document the medical necessity for hospitalization.

14. Write each note so that the sections are consistent and support the bill. For example, diagnosis codes and procedure codes must be compatible.

    For example:

    a) There should be no bills for Level 4 or 5 office visits with the diagnosis code for viral conjunctivitis and supported by a two-line progress note.

b) If ordering diagnostic testing, each test should correlate with the diagnoses stated in the note and should be medically necessary for at least one diagnosis listed.

c) The exam should be appropriate to the chief complaint and chronic illnesses.

15. Write each note with attention not only to supporting the bill, but to meeting the standard of care in choice of diagnosis, treatment and follow-up. For example, if conducting a counseling visit, little detail is required to support the bill. However, detail may be required to demonstrate that the practitioner has met the standard of care. To save time and minimize professional liability, refer in progress notes to patient instruction sheets, if the practice has them. For example, if spending 20 minutes of a 25-minute visit counseling a diabetic patient on dietary compliance, write "Counseled on diabetic diet, visit 10 a.m. to 10:25 a.m. Patient Instruction Sheet 101." As long as the practice has an appropriate patient instruction sheet 101, the clinician has documented sufficiently to defend a malpractice action alleging that the patient was not properly instructed.

ADDITIONAL RESOURCES

Reimbursement for nurse practitioner services

Buppert, C. "Safe, smart billing and coding for evaluation and management," an educational module on compact disk from the Law Office of Carolyn Buppert. Order from www.buppert.com.

Buppert, C. (2005). *The Primary Care Provider's Guide to Compensation and Quality: How to get paid and not get sued.* Jones & Bartlett Publishers. Sudbury, MA.

Coding

Physicians Current Procedural Terminology [for the current year]. American Medical Association, Chicago.

ICD-9: International Classification of Diseases, 9th edition. American Medical Association, Chicago.

Useful web sites

For the Code of Federal Regulations (CFR)
   http://www.gpoaccess.gov/cfr
For the Medicare Manuals
   http://www.cms.hhs.gov/manuals

APPENDIX A

NON-PHYSICIAN PRACTITIONER
QUESTIONS AND ANSWERS

Related Change Request (CR) #: N/A

Related CR Release Date: N/A

Effective Date: N/A - This is informational only.

Medlearn Matters Number: SE0418

Revised

Non-Physician Practitioner Questions and Answers

Note: This article was revised on August 16, 2005. The only change was the answer (A14) to question 14 (Q14) on page 4. All other information remains the same.

Provider Types Affected

Non-Physician Practitioners (NPPs), physicians, suppliers, and providers

Provider Action Needed

Be sure to understand the policies related to services for Skilled Nursing Facilities (SNF) and Nursing Facilities (NF) as they relate to Non-Physician Practitioners.

Background

The Balanced Budget Act of 1997 modified the way the Medicare program pays for Non-Physician Practitioner (NPP) services. Prior to January 1, 1998, these services were reimbursed by Medicare Part B only in certain geographical areas and health care settings. The Balanced Budget Act removed the restrictions on settings and effective January 1998, payment is allowed for non-physician practitioner services in all geographic areas and health care settings permitted under State licensing laws.

On November 13, 2003, CMS issued the Survey & Certification letter (S&C-04-08), which addresses the differences in requirements concerning the delegation of physician tasks in Skilled Nursing Facilities (SNFs) and Nursing Facilities (NFs) from a survey and certification perspective. Please note that reimbursement requirements for NPPs may differ from the survey and certification requirements. The following questions (Q1 through Q17) have been asked by NPPs, and each question has been answered (A1 through A17) by the Centers for Medicare & Medicaid Services (CMS).

Q1. Why do new regulations from CMS governing physician delegation of services differ between Skilled Nursing Facilities (SNFs) and Nursing Facilities (NFs)?
A1. The requirements addressing physician delegation of services are not new. The distinction made between the delegation of physician visits and tasks between SNFs and NFs is mandated by Congress in the law.

The original authority for 42 Code of Federal Regulations (CFR) § 483.40 was the sentence in section 1819(b)(6)(A) of the Social Security Act requiring that every SNF resident's medical care be under the supervision of a physician (the same sentence appeared in section 1919(b)(6)(A) of the Social Security Act for NFs). The requirements contained in 42 CFR, § 483.40, include a prescribed visit schedule and the requirement for the physician to perform the initial visit personally.

Section 483.40 of the CFR originally applied these same standards uniformly in both SNFs and NFs. However, in section 4801(d) of the Omnibus Budget Reconciliation Act of 1990 (OBRA '90), Congress subsequently amended the Medicaid provisions of the law (section 1919(b)(6)(A) of the Social Security Act) to allow, at the option of the State, all physician tasks (including the initial visit) to be delegated to physician extenders who are not employed by the facility but who are working in collaboration with the physician. In response, CMS amended the regulations to reflect this broader authority for delegating physician tasks in NFs (see § 483.40(f)). Since Congress declined to make a similar change in the statutory requirements for SNFs at section 1819(b)(6)(A) of the Social Security Act, the corresponding SNF requirements in § 483.40(c) and (e) remain unchanged.

Q2. When may non-physician practitioners (NPPs) begin to bill for medically necessary visits that occur prior to the initial comprehensive visit in a SNF and in a NF?
A2. CMS defined "initial comprehensive visit" in the November 13, 2003 S&C-04-08 and stated that NPPs may perform any medically necessary visits even if they occur prior to the initial comprehensive visits in both SNFs and NFs. Medically necessary visits that NPPs perform on or after November 13, 2003, may be billed to the carrier when collaboration and billing requirements are met in the SNF and NF setting. The Survey & Certification letter S&C-04-08, may be found at:

http://www.cms.hhs.gov/medicaid/survey-cert/letters.asp

Q3. If State regulations require a physician co-signature for orders and/or notes written by an NPP, may the physician bill for this action?
A3. No. CMS only pays for medically necessary face-to-face visits by the physician or NPP with the resident. Since the NPP is performing the medically necessary visit, the NPP would bill for the visit.

Q4. If State regulations require more frequent visits than those that are federally mandated, are NPPs able to bill for those visits?
A4. CMS only reimburses physicians and NPPs for medically necessary visits and federally prescribed visits. Visits required to fulfill or meet State requirements are considered administrative requirements and are not medically necessary for the resident. Medicare pays for services that are reasonable and medically necessary for the treatment of illness or injury only, as stated in the Social Security Act, section 1862(a)(1)(A).

Q5. May NPPs who are employed by the facility bill for medically necessary visits?
A5. Payment may be made for the services of Nurse Practitioners (NPs) and Clinical Nurse Specialists (CNSs) who are employed by a SNF or NF when their services are rendered to facility residents. If NPs and CNSs employed by a facility opt to reassign payment for their professional services to the facility, the facility can bill the appropriate Medicare Part B carrier under the NPs' or CNSs' PINs for their professional services. Otherwise, the NPs or CNSs who are employed by a SNF or NF bill the carrier directly for their services to facility residents.

On the other hand, Physician Assistants (PAs) who are employed by a SNF or NF cannot reassign payment for their professional services to the facility because Medicare law requires the employer of a PA to bill for the PA's services. Hence, the facility must always bill the Part B carrier under the PA's PIN for the PA's professional services to facility residents.

Q6. May NPPs employed by the NF perform the initial comprehensive visit, sign initial orders, or perform other federally required visits in NFs?
A6. No. The statute specifies that the NPPs are prohibited from providing these services when **employed** by the facility. The Social Security Act states at section 1919(b)(6)(A) that the health care of every resident must be provided under the supervision of a physician or under the supervision of an NPP **not** employed by the facility who is working in collaboration with a physician.

Q7. May NPPs perform the initial comprehensive visit in SNFs?
A7. No. The Social Security Act states at Section 1819(b)(6)(A) "that the medical care of every resident must be provided under the supervision of a physician." Congress did not extend this benefit to NPPs in an SNF as was done under 1919(b)(6)(A).

Q8. When may NPPs sign the initial orders for a SNF resident?
A8. NPPs may not sign initial orders for an SNF resident. However, they may write initial orders for a resident (only) when they review those orders with the attending physician in person or via telephone conversation and have the orders signed by the physician.

Q9 Must a physician verify and sign orders written by an NPP who is employed by the NF?
A9. Yes. The regulation at 42 CFR, § 483.40(b)(3) states, the physician must "Sign and date all orders with the exception of influenza and pneumococcal polysaccharide vaccines, which may be administered per physician-approved facility policy after an assessment for contraindications."

In accordance with 42 CFR, Section 483.40(f), required physician tasks, such as verifying and signing orders in an NF, can be delegated under certain circumstances to a physician assistant, nurse practitioner, or clinical nurse specialist who is **not** an employee of the facility but who is working in collaboration with a physician. Therefore, in order to comply with survey and certification requirements, the physician must sign all orders written by an NPP who **is** employed by the NF.

Q10. Why must a physician verify and sign orders written by an NPP in the SNF?
A10. In SNFs, depending on State law and the facility's policy, physicians do NOT have to verify and sign orders written by an NPP after the initial comprehensive visit. Nonetheless, the ultimate responsibility for delegated tasks remains with the physician, as indicated in § 483.40(e)(1)(iii). For a NF, depending upon State law, NPPs not employed by the facility but who are working in collaboration with a physician are not required to have their orders (initial or ongoing) cosigned by a physician.

Q11. Referring to S&C –04-08 issued on November 13, 2003, the chart under the "Other Medically Necessary Visits and Orders" column, it specifies the ability of the NPP to perform AND sign but in the column for "Other Required Visits" it does not address signing. Does CMS require a physician's signature in such cases?
A11. 'Other Required Visits' refers to the federally required visits. During these required visits, it is not always necessary to write orders. However, during a "Medically Necessary Visit," which is when the resident's condition may have changed, thus, warranting a visit outside the federally required schedule, the resident is exhibiting signs and/or symptoms that require medical attention. In these cases, CMS believes orders will often be required and, thus, expect orders to address the resident's change in condition.

Therefore, an NPP may sign the medically required orders. Please remain mindful that the survey and certification requirement that the physician must sign and date all orders remains in effect. (See Q&As 9 & 10.)

Q12. Why can't a PA, regardless of employment, sign certifications/re-certifications for SNF residents?
A12. Congress amended section 1814(a)(2) of the Social Security Act in 1989. The Social Security Act specifies that NPs and CNSs who are not employed by the facility may certify (and recertify) that the services the beneficiary requires may only be performed in the SNF. They did not extend this benefit to PAs. Therefore, by statute, PAs may not sign SNF certifications/re-certifications.

Q13. If a physician extender is not employed by the NF but is employed by an organization related to the NF, may he/she still provide services in the nursing home?
A13. The requirement in 42 CFR, § 483.40(f), is specific in that the physician tasks may be performed by a NP, PA, or CNS "who is not an employee of the facility." In this case, the NPP is not an employee of the NF and, thus, can perform physician tasks as long as they work in collaboration with the physician.

Q14. If an NP or CNS is not employed by the SNF but is employed by an organization related to the SNF, may he/she sign the certification and re-certifications?
A14. The requirement in 42 CFR § 424.20(e) is specific in that an NP or CNS "neither of whom has a direct or indirect employment relationship with the facility" may sign the certifications and re-certifications. Under 42 CFR 424.20(e)(2)(ii), when an NP or CNS has a direct employment relationship (as defined under common law) with an entity other than the SNF itself, he or she is also considered to have an indirect employment relationship with the SNF in any instance where the employing entity has an agreement with the SNF for the provision of general nursing services. For further explanation of this provision, please refer to the FY 2006 SNF prospective payment system final rule, 70 FR 45035 - 36, August 4, 2005. (Social Security Act section 1814(a)(2))

Q15. If physician delegation responsibilities are based on payment source, what are the physician delegation responsibilities for private pay resident, VA contracts or managed care?
A15. If the resident's stay is being paid for by a source other than Medicare or Medicaid AND the resident is residing in a Medicare/Medicaid dually-certified facility, follow the most stringent requirement. If the resident is residing in a Medicare only or a Medicaid only certified facility, then follow the requirements for that specific certified facility.

Q16. Are NPPs allowed to certify/recertify therapy plans of care under Medicare Part B?
A16. 42 CFR § 424.24(c)(3) states that if a physician or NPP establishes the plan of care, he/she must also certify the plan of care. If the plan of care is established by a physical or occupational therapist or speech language pathologist, a physician or NPP who has knowledge of the case must sign the plan of care. (This Q&A was not addressed in the November 13, 2003, Survey & Certification letter, S&C-04-08.)

Should you have any questions concerning this article, please submit your inquiry via the CMS Web site as follows:

1) Click on Feedback in top tool bar of http://www.cms.hhs.gov (from Home page or any page on cms.hhs.gov).

2) Select and click "Site Feedback" in last paragraph.

3) User should:

    a. Enter his/her email address;

    b. At Category, select "Providers" from the drop down menu;

    c. At the sub-category, select Nursing Home Quality Initiative;

    d. Enter feedback in space provided; and

    e. Submit feedback.

Related Instructions

The CMS Web site contains considerable information regarding SNF billing procedures and NPP billing processes. Some of the specific sites are as follows:

The *Medicare Claims Processing Manual, Pub. 100-04, Chapter 7 (SNF Part B Billing (Including Inpatient Part B and Outpatient Fee Schedule))* can be found at the following CMS Website:

http://www.cms.hhs.gov/manuals/104_claims/clm104c07.pdf

The *Skilled Nursing Facility Manual, Chapter V (Billing Procedures)* is located at the following CMS Website:

http://www.cms.hhs.gov/manuals/12_snf/sn500.asp

The Home Health Agency Manual, Chapter IV (Billing Procedures) Website is located at:

http://www.cms.hhs.gov/manuals/11_hha/hh400.asp.

Additional Information

The CMS Quarterly Provider Update Websites for Non-Physician Practitioners (NPPs) for 2004 can be found at:

http://www.cms.hhs.gov/providerupdate/january2004/nonphys.asp

http://www.cms.hhs.gov/providerupdate/april2004/nonphys.asp

http://www.cms.hhs.gov/providerupdate/July2004/nonphys.asp

http://www.cms.hhs.gov/providerupdate/october2004/nonphys.asp

In addition, the CMS Quarterly Provider Update Websites for NPPs for 2003 can be found at:

http://www.cms.hhs.gov/providerupdate/january2003/nonphys.asp

http://www.cms.hhs.gov/providerupdate/april2003/nonphys.asp

http://www.cms.hhs.gov/providerupdate/july2003/nonphys.asp

http://www.cms.hhs.gov/providerupdate/october2003/nonphys.asp

Related Change Request #: N/A	Medlearn Matters Number: SE0418

Acronyms	
CFR = Code of Federal Regulations	OBRA '90 = Omnibus Budget Reconciliation Act of 1990
CMS = Centers for Medicare & Medicaid Services	PA = Physician Assistant
CNS = Clinical Nurse Specialist	S&C = Survey & Certification
NF = Nursing Facility	SNF = Skilled Nursing Facility
NP = Nurse Practitioner	VA = Veterans Administration
NPP = Non-Physician Practitioner (NPs, CNSs, & PAs are considered NPPs)	

APPENDIX B

CMS MEMORANDUM: PHYSICIAN DELEGATION OF TASKS IN SKILLED NURSING FACILITIES (SNFs) AND NURSING FACILITIES (NFs)

DEPARTMENT OF HEALTH & HUMAN SERVICES
Centers for Medicare & Medicaid Services
7500 Security Boulevard, Mail Stop S2-12-25
Baltimore, Maryland 21244-1850

Center for Medicaid and State Operations/Survey and Certification Group

Ref: S&C-04-08

DATE: **November 13, 2003**

TO: State Survey Agency Directors

FROM: Director
Survey and Certification Group

SUBJECT: Physician Delegation of Tasks in Skilled Nursing Facilities (SNFs) and
Nursing Facilities (NFs)

The purpose of this memorandum is to clarify for State survey agencies and providers the
regulatory differences concerning physician delegation of tasks in SNFs and NFs. The
distinction in policies between these two settings (SNFs and NFs) is based in statute. Inaccurate
interpretation of these regulations may affect compliance and may also affect payment to
providers. The key to accurate interpretation is identifying what setting, SNF or NF, the
physician services are being provided. Table 1, which summarizes these delegations, is provided
at the end. This memorandum addresses the issue of the authority of physician extenders to: 1)
perform physician visits and write orders; and 2) sign certifications and re-certifications in SNFs
and NFs.

**This memorandum replaces Survey and Certification memorandum S&C-03-18 dated
April 10, 2003, which discusses physician delegation of tasks in SNFs and NFs. Please
disregard the April 10 version.**

Physician Delegation of Tasks in Skilled Nursing Facilities.

Under the requirements for long term care facilities, the regulations at 42 C.F.R. 483.40(e) state
that, "A physician may not delegate a task when the regulations specify that the physician must
perform it personally, or when the delegation is prohibited under State law or by the facility's
own policies."

Physician and other Medically Necessary Visits in SNFs: The initial comprehensive visit in a
SNF is the initial visit during which the physician completes a thorough assessment, develops a
plan of care and writes or verifies admitting orders for the resident. Under the regulations at 42
C.F.R. 483.40(c)(1), the initial comprehensive visit must occur no later than 30 days after
admission. Further, under 42 C.F.R. 483.40(c)(4) and (e), the physician may not delegate the
initial comprehensive visit in a SNF. Non-physician practitioners may perform other medically
necessary visits prior to and after the physician initial comprehensive visit.

Page 2 –State Survey Agency Directors

Once the physician has completed the initial comprehensive visit in the SNF, the physician may then delegate alternate visits to a Physician Assistant (PA), Nurse Practitioner (NP), or Clinical Nurse Specialist (CNS) who is licensed as such by the State and performing within the scope of practice in that State, as required under 42 C.F.R. 483.40(c)(4).

Certifications/Re-certifications in SNFs: Under the SNF regulations at 42 C.F.R. 424.20, certifications and re-certifications are required to verify that a resident requires daily skilled nursing care or rehabilitation services. 42 C.F.R. 424.20(e)(2) (which reflects the requirements of the law at section 1814 (a)(2) of the Social Security Act) states that NPs and CNSs who are not employed by the facility and are working in collaboration with a physician, when permitted under the scope of practice for the State, may sign the required initial certification and re-certifications. By contrast, PAs (regardless of employment) and those NPs and CNSs who are employed by the facility do not have authority to sign initial certifications or the SNF required recertifications.

Performance of Physician Tasks in Nursing Facilities.

Physician and Other Medically Necessary Visits in NFs: The initial comprehensive visit in a NF is the same as in a SNF. That is, the initial comprehensive visit is the initial visit during which the physician completes a thorough assessment, develops a plan of care and writes or verifies admitting orders for the resident, which must take place no later than 30 days after admission. The regulations at 42 C.F.R. 483.40(f) state that "At the option of the State, any required physician task in a NF (including tasks which the regulations specify must be performed personally by the physician) may also be satisfied when performed by a nurse practitioner, clinical nurse specialist, or physician assistant who is not an employee of the facility but who is working in collaboration with a physician." In other words, non-physician practitioners that have a direct relationship with a physician and who are not employed by the facility may perform the initial comprehensive visit, any other required physician visit and other medically necessary visits for a resident of a NF as the State allows. Non-physician practitioners may also perform other medically necessary visits prior to and after the physician initial comprehensive visit.

At the option of the State, NPs, PAs, and CNSs who are employees of the facility, while not permitted to perform visits required under the schedule prescribed at 42 C.F.R. 483.40(c)(1), are permitted to perform other medically necessary visits and write orders based on these visits. The physician must verify and sign any orders written by non-physician practitioners who are employed by the facility. For example, if a resident complains of a headache, the NP, CNS, or PA employed by the facility may assess the resident and write orders to address the condition. The physician must then verify and sign the orders. However, these medically necessary visits performed by NPs, CNSs, and PAs employed by the facility may not take the place of the physician required visits, nor may the visit count towards meeting the required physician visit schedule prescribed at 42 C.F.R. 483.40(c)(1).

Dually Certified Facilities.

While the CFR does not address dually certified SNF/NFs directly, the CFR is clear about who can perform tasks in a SNF and in a NF. In a facility where beds are dually certified, the facility must determine how the resident stay is being paid. For residents in a Part A Medicare stay, the PA, NP, and CNS must follow the guidelines for services in a SNF.

Page 3 –State Survey Agency Directors

For Medicaid stays, the PA, NP, and CNS must follow the provisions outlined for care in NFs. As such, in a dually certified nursing home, any required physician task for a Medicaid beneficiary in a NF certified bed, at the option of the State, may be performed by a NP, CNS, or PA who is not an employee of the facility but who is working in collaboration with a physician. In addition, in a dually certified nursing home and at the option of a physician, required physician visits for a Medicare beneficiary in a SNF certified bed may be alternated between personal visits by the physician and visits by a PA, CNS, or NP after the physician makes the initial first visit.

Table 1 below summarizes the requirements for non-physician practitioners to perform visits, sign orders, and sign certifications and recertifications, when this function is permitted under the scope of practice for the State.

Table 1: Authority for Non-physician Practitioners to Perform Visits, Sign Orders and Sign Certifications/Recertifications When Permitted by the State*

	Initial Comprehensive Visit /Orders	Other Required Visits^	Other Medically Necessary Visits & Orders+	Certification/ Recertification
SNFs				
NP & CNS employed by the facility	May not perform/ May not sign	May perform	May perform and sign	May not sign
NP & CNS not a facility employee	May not perform/ May not sign	May perform	May perform and sign	May sign subject to State Requirements
PA regardless of employer	May not perform/ May not sign	May perform	May perform and sign	May not sign
NFs				
NP, CNS & PA employed by the facility	May not perform/ May not sign	May not perform	May perform and sign	May sign subject to State Requirements
NP, CNS & PA not a facility employee	May perform/ May sign	May perform	May perform and sign	May sign subject to State Requirements

*This reflects clinical practice guidelines
^Other required visits are the required monthly visits that may be alternated between physician and non-physician practitioner after the initial comprehensive visit is completed
+Medically necessary visits may be performed prior to the initial comprehensive visit

Page 4 –State Survey Agency Directors

Effective Date: This policy is in effect immediately.

Training: This policy should be shared with all appropriate survey and certification staff, their managers, and the state/regional office training coordinator.

/s/
Thomas E. Hamilton

cc: Survey and Certification Regional Office Management (G-5)

APPENDIX C

NURSE PRACTITIONER SERVICES
UNDER MEDICARE HOSPICE

Program Memorandum Intermediaries	Department of Health & Human Services (DHHS) Centers for Medicare & Medicaid Services (CMS)
Transmittal A-03-053	Date: JUNE 20, 2003

CHANGE REQUEST 2750

SUBJECT: Nurse Practitioner Services Under Medicare Hospice

Purpose

The purpose of this Program Memorandum (PM) is to clarify the policy and interpretation for services provided by nurse practitioners (NP) under the Medicare hospice benefit. Since hospice is a Medicare Part A benefit, this PM does not apply to Part B.

Introduction

We have received numerous questions regarding the role of an NP in the provision of services to beneficiaries who have elected the hospice benefit. Numerous Medicare statutory and regulatory provisions affect the determination of services that may or may not be provided by an NP. These provisions are described in the following sections.

Physicians
The law is explicit as to the role of a physician in Medicare's hospice benefit. §1861(r)(1) of the Social Security Act (Act) defines the term physician as "… a doctor of medicine or osteopathy legally authorized to practice medicine and surgery by the state in which he performs such function or action…" Section 1861(dd)(3)(B) of the Act defines the attending physician as the physician (as defined in subsection (r)(1) … "whom the individual identifies as having the most significant role in the determination and delivery of medical care to the individual…"

Nurse Practitioner
The law is explicit as to the role of the NP in Medicare. Nurse practitioners are identified in §1861(s)(K)(i) of the Act which stipulates, "… services which would be physicians' services if furnished by a physician (as defined in subsection (r)(l) and which are performed by a nurse practitioner …(as defined in subsection (aa)(5) working in collaboration (as defined in subsection (aa)(6) with a physician (as defined in subsection (r)(l), which the nurse practitioner … is legally authorized to perform by the State in which the services are performed and such services as would be covered under subparagraph (A) if furnished incident to a physician's professional service, but only if no facility or other provider charges or is paid any amounts with respect to the furnishing of such services…" Section 1861(aa)(5)(A) of the Act defines the nurse practitioner as "…an individual who is legally authorized to perform (in the State in which they perform such services) in accordance with State law (or the State regulatory mechanism provided by State law), and who meets such training, education and experience requirements (or any combination thereof) as …prescribed in regulation." Section 1861(aa)(6) defines collaboration as "… a process in which an NP works with a physician to deliver healthcare services within the scope of the practitioner's professional expertise, with medical direction and appropriate supervision as provided for in jointly developed guidelines or other mechanisms as defined by the law of the State in which the services are performed."

Medicare regulations are implicit as to the role of an NP in the Medicare hospice benefit since the only references made are to registered nurses. No explicit references are made to nurse practitioners. Section1861(dd)(2)(B) of the Act describes the interdisciplinary group as "… personnel which (i) includes at least (II) one registered professional nurse…" 42 CFR 418 delineates and describes nursing care however, it is silent to the advanced practice role.

CMS-Pub 60A

2

Sections 4511 and 4512 of the Balanced Budget Act (BBA) of 1997 removed the restrictions on the type of areas and settings in which Medicare pays for the professional services of the NPs. Payments are allowed for services furnished by NPs in all areas and settings permitted under applicable state licensure laws, but only if no facility or other provider charges or is paid any amounts with respect to the furnishing of such professional services.

Plan of Care (POC)
Medicare regulation explicitly requires a physician to perform certain services, such as establishing the POC and its periodic review as defined in §1861(dd) of the Act. A physician is defined in §1861(r)(l) as a doctor of medicine or osteopathy. Section 1861(dd)(l) further delineates that items and services that are provided for beneficiaries under the hospice benefit must be " … under a written plan (for providing such care to an individual) established and periodically reviewed by the individual's attending physician and by the medical director (and by the interdisciplinary group described in paragraph (2)(B)." Federal Regulations at 42 CFR 418.58 indicate that the POC must be established and updated by the attending physician, the medical director or physician designee and the interdisciplinary group (IDG). 42 CFR 418.68(a) stipulates that the IDG be comprised of at least a physician, a registered nurse, a social worker, and a pastoral or other counselor.

Conclusion

Since Medicare regulations do not specifically provide that only a physician may write orders for beneficiaries electing the Medicare hospice benefit, if State law permits NPs to see, treat and write orders for patients, and if they are employed by a hospice agency, they may perform these activities for beneficiaries electing the hospice benefit. In addition, there is nothing that precludes a hospice from employing an NP.

The services provided by the NP would include those recognized and accepted by the State in which the services are provided and which are not excluded by Federal regulation. In addition, the NP role and responsibilities would need to be defined in the beneficiary's plan of care.

Nurse practitioners may not certify or re-certify that a beneficiary has a terminal diagnosis with a prognosis of 6 months or less if the illness or disease runs its usual course. Nurse practitioners may not take the place of the physician on the IDG but can fill the role of the registered nurse.

The law allows for a separate Medicare Part B payment to be made for services of a beneficiary's attending physician if he or she is not an employee of or under contract to a hospice. Since NPs are not physicians pursuant to §1861(r) (1) they may not act as attending physicians.

Since the hospice benefit is a prospective payment system with an all-inclusive daily rate in exchange for the provision of requisite services, which includes nursing and some physician services payment methodology, separate billing for NP services would not be permitted under Medicare Part A.

Provider Education

Intermediaries must share the information in this PM with providers through a posting on their Web site within two weeks and publish this information in their next regularly scheduled bulletin.

The *effective date* for this PM is July 1, 2003.

The *implementation date* for this PM is July 1, 2003.

These instructions should be implemented within your current operating budget.

This PM may be discarded June 20, 2004.

If you have any questions, contact Terri Deutsch at 410-786-9462.

APPENDIX D

NURSE PRACTITIONER
IS ATTENDING PHYSICIAN IN HOSPICE, MEDICARE CLAIMS PROCESSING MANUAL CHAPTER 11

Payment for physicians' administrative and general supervisory activities is included in the hospice payment rates. These activities include participating in the establishment, review and updating of plans of care, supervising care and services and establishing governing policies.

These activities are generally performed by the physician serving as the medical director and the physician member of the interdisciplinary group (IDG). Nurse practitioners may not serve as or replace the medical director or physician member of the IDG.

40.1.2 - Patient Care Services

(Rev. 304, Issued: 09-24-04, Effective: 12-08-03, Implementation: 06-28-04)

Payment for physicians or nurse practitioner serving as the attending physician, who provide direct patient care services and who are hospice employees or under arrangement with the hospice, is made in the following manner:

- Hospices establish a charge and bill the FI for these services.

- The FI pays the hospice at the lesser of the actual charge or 100 percent of the Medicare physician fee schedule for physician services or 85% of the fee schedule amount for nurse practitioner services. This payment is in addition to the daily hospice rates.

- Payment for physician and nurse practitioner services is counted with the payments made at the daily payment rates to determine whether the overall hospice cap amount has been exceeded.

- No payment is made for physician or nurse practitioner services furnished voluntarily. However, some physicians and nurse practitioners may seek payment for certain services while furnishing other services on a volunteer basis. Payment may be made for services not furnished voluntarily if the hospice is obligated to pay the physician or nurse practitioner for the services. A physician or nurse practitioner must treat Medicare patients on the same basis as other patients in the hospice; a physician or nurse practitioner may not designate all services rendered to non-Medicare patients as volunteer and at the same time bill the hospice for services rendered to Medicare patients.

- No payment is made for nurse practitioner services that can be performed by a registered nurse, nor is payment made for nurse practitioner services that are performed outside of the attending physician role. Nurse practitioner services are generally encompassed in the per diem payment rate. The only payment that can be made for services of a nurse practitioner is made for services furnished in the role of an attending physician.

    EXAMPLE: Dr. Jones has an agreement with a hospice to serve as its medical director on a volunteer basis. Dr. Jones does not furnish any direct patient care services on a volunteer basis. A Medicare beneficiary enters the hospice and designates Dr. Jones as her attending physician. When he furnishes a direct service to the beneficiary, he bills the hospice for this service and the hospice in turn bills the FI and is paid for the service. Dr. Jones may not bill Medicare Part B as an independent attending physician because as a volunteer he is deemed to be a hospice employee.

40.1.3 - Attending Physician Services

(Rev. 304, Issued: 09-24-04, Effective: 12-08-03, Implementation: 06-28-04)

When hospice coverage is elected, the beneficiary waives all rights to Medicare Part B payments for professional services that are related to the treatment and management of his/her terminal illness during any period his/her hospice benefit election is in force, except for professional services of an "attending physician," who is not an employee of the designated hospice nor receives compensation from the hospice for those services. For purposes of administering the hospice benefit provisions, an "attending physician" means an individual who:

- Is a doctor of medicine or osteopathy or

- A nurse practitioner (for professional services related to the terminal illness that are furnished on or after December 8, 2003); and

- Is identified by the individual, at the time he/she elects hospice coverage, as having the most significant role in the determination and delivery of their medical care.

Even though a beneficiary elects hospice coverage, he/she may designate and use an attending physician, who is not employed by nor receives compensation from the hospice for professional services furnished, in addition to the services of hospice-employed physicians. The professional services of an attending physician, who may be a nurse practitioner as defined in Chapter 9, that are reasonable and necessary for the treatment and management of a hospice patient's terminal illness are not considered hospice services.

Where the service is considered a hospice service (i.e., a service related to the hospice patient's terminal illness that was furnished by someone other than the designated "attending physician" [or a physician substituting for the attending physician]) the physician or other provider must look to the hospice for payment.

Professional services related to the hospice patient's terminal condition that were furnished by the "attending physician", who may be a nurse practitioner, are billed to carriers. When the attending physician furnishes a terminal illness related service that includes both a professional and technical component (e.g., x-rays), he/she bills the professional component of such services to the carrier and looks to the hospice for payment for the technical component. Likewise, the attending physician, who may be a nurse practitioner, would look to the hospice for payment for terminal illness related services furnished that have no professional component (e.g., clinical lab tests). The remainder of this section explains this in greater detail.

When a Medicare beneficiary elects hospice coverage he/she may designate an attending physician, who may be a nurse practitioner, not employed by the hospice, in addition to receiving care from hospice-employed physicians. The professional services of a non-hospice affiliated attending physician for the treatment and management of a hospice patient's terminal illness are not considered "hospice services." These attending physician services are billed to the carrier, provided they were not furnished under a payment arrangement with the hospice. The attending physician codes services with the GV modifier "Attending physician not employed or paid under agreement by the patient's hospice provider" when billing his/her professional services furnished for the treatment and management of a hospice patient's terminal condition. Carriers make payment to the attending physician or beneficiary, as appropriate, based on the payment and deductible rules applicable to each covered service.

Payments for the services of attending physician are not counted in determining whether the hospice cap amount has been exceeded because services provided by an independent attending physician are not part of the hospice's care.

Services provided by an independent attending physician who may be a nurse practitioner must be coordinated with any direct care services provided by hospice physicians.

Only the direct professional services of an independent attending physician, who may be a nurse practitioner, to a patient may be billed; the costs for services such as lab or x-rays are not to be included in the bill.

If another physician covers for a hospice patient's designated attending physician, the services of the substituting physician are billed by the designated attending physician under the reciprocal or locum tenens billing instructions. In such instances, the attending physician bills using the GV modifier in conjunction with either the Q5 or Q6 modifier.

When services related to a hospice patient's terminal condition are furnished under a payment arrangement with the hospice by the designated attending physician who may be a nurse practitioner, the physician must look to the hospice for payment. In this situation the physicians' services are hospice services and are billed by the hospice to its FI.

Carriers must process and pay for covered, medically necessary Part B services that physicians furnish to patients after their hospice benefits are revoked even if the patient remains under the care of the hospice. Such services are billed without the GV or GW modifiers. Make payment based on applicable Medicare payment and deductible rules for each covered service even if the beneficiary continues to be treated by the hospice after hospice benefits are revoked.

The CWF response contains the period of hospice entitlement. This information is a permanent part of the notice and is furnished on all CWF replies and automatic notices.